Learn Korean For Beginners Master the Language Through Practice Exercises

30 Essential Topics with Grammar Reviews, Writing Drills, and Answer Keys for Beginners and Self-Learners

By Jennie Lee

Find other books from Jennie Lee and Polyscholar

www.polyscholar.com

Contents

Introduction

Welcome to <u>Korean Language Practice: 30 Essential Topics for Learners</u>, a companion workbook designed to help reinforce your understanding of foundational Korean grammar and vocabulary through hands-on practice. Whether you are currently learning Korean or have already completed a course, this book offers an opportunity to actively apply what you've learned and build confidence in your skills.

This workbook was developed by Jennie Lee, author of <u>Learn Korean Workbook for Beginners</u> and <u>Learn Korean Grammar</u>. Drawing on the structure and lessons from those two core texts, this volume focuses entirely on practice. Across 30 chapters, you'll find hundreds of targeted exercises designed to help you strengthen your reading, writing, and comprehension of key grammar patterns and language functions.

Each chapter focuses on a practical topic such as introducing yourself, making plans, giving directions, or talking about the weather. For every topic, you'll begin with a one-page grammar summary to review essential rules and structures. This is followed by 20 exercises ranging from sentence completion and translation to short dialogues and paragraph writing. To support self-study, each chapter also includes a full answer key so you can check your work and continue progressing at your own pace.

This workbook does not include stroke order or Hangul instruction, and assumes you already know how to read Korean. It is meant to be used alongside your other learning resources, helping you transition from recognition to fluency through repetition, review, and real-world context.

If you want to learn for reinforce your knowledge of stroke order visit our website www.polyscholar.com for Jennie Lees Learn Korean for Beginners which goes into detail on how to draw the Hangual characters.

We hope this book becomes a valuable part of your Korean learning journey. 꾸준히 공부하세요 — studying steadily — and enjoy each step forward!

Jennie Lee

Introducing Yourself
Grammar Review

This chapter focuses on the basic structures used when introducing yourself in Korean. Below are key grammar rules and expressions commonly used in self-introductions:

1. Subject Marker – 은/는
Used to mark the subject of the sentence.

Example: 저는 학생입니다. ((As for me,) I am a student.)

2. The Copula – 입니다 / 입니까?

입니다 is the formal declarative ending meaning "to be."

입니까? is the formal question form.

Example: 저는 미국 사람입니다. (I am American.)

Example: (당신은) 선생님입니까? (Are you a teacher?)

3. Name Introduction – 이름 + 예요 / 이에요

예요 is used when the name ends in a vowel; 이에요 when it ends in a consonant.

Example: 제 이름은 민수예요. (My name is Minsu.)

4. Nationality – Country + 사람

Use the country name followed by 사람 to indicate nationality.

Example: 저는 일본 사람이에요. (I am Japanese.)

5. Polite Greetings
- 안녕하세요: Hello (polite)

- 만나서 반갑습니다: Nice to meet you (formal)

These structures form the foundation of a polite and basic self-introduction in Korean. Practice using the correct sentence endings and topic markers to sound natural and respectful.

Exercises: Introducing Yourself

1. Fill in the blank: 안녕하세요! 저는 _____입니다.

2. Fill in the blank: 제 이름은 _____예요/이에요.

3. Choose the correct particle: 저(은/는) 미국 사람입니다.

4. Rearrange the words: 입니다. / 저는 / 학생

5. Fill in the blank: 저는 _____에서 왔어요.

6. Choose the correct form: (이에요/예요) for the name '민수'

7. Translate into Korean: I am a teacher.

8. Translate into Korean: Nice to meet you.

9. Match the phrases:

   a. 만나서 반갑습니다.   ( ) I'm a doctor.

   b. 저는 의사입니다.   ( ) Nice to meet you.

   c. 제 이름은 수지예요.   ( ) My name is Suji.

10. Fill in the blank with an appropriate country + 사람: 저는 _____ 사람입니다.

11. Correct the mistake: 제 이름은 민수입니다예요.

12. Answer the question: (당신은) 선생님입니까? (Answer in Korean)

13. Create a short dialogue between two people meeting for the first time.

14. Choose the appropriate response: 만나서 반갑습니다 → ( ) 저도 반갑습니다 / ( ) 아니요

15. Complete the introduction: 안녕하세요. 제 이름은 _____. (Or 저는 _____) 만나서 반갑습니다.

16. Write your own formal self-introduction (3–4 lines in Korean).

17. Identify the subject marker: 저는 학생입니다.

18. Fill in: A: _____ B: 안녕하세요. (Use greeting expression)

19. Fill in: 제 _____은/는 철수예요. (Use family or personal relation)

20. Match the Korean to English professions:
   a. 선생님   ( ) teacher
   b. 학생   ( ) student
   c. 의사   ( ) doctor

Introducing Yourself – Answer Key

1. 안녕하세요! 저는 민수입니다. / 안녕하세요! 저는 수지입니다.

2. 제 이름은 민수예요. / 제 이름은 철수예요.

3. 저는 미국 사람입니다.

4. 저는 학생입니다.

5. 저는 한국에서 왔어요. / 저는 일본에서 왔어요.

6. 예요 (민수 ends in a vowel)   7. 저는 선생님입니다.

8. 만나서 반갑습니다.   9. a-2, b-1, c-3

10. 저는 한국 사람입니다. / 저는 중국 사람입니다.

11. 제 이름은 민수입니다예요. → Correct: 제 이름은 민수예요. Or 제 이름은 민수입니다.

12. 네, 선생님입니다. / 아니요, 학생입니다.

13. A: 안녕하세요. 저는 민수입니다. 만나서 반갑습니다.

   B: 안녕하세요. 저는 수지예요. 저도 반갑습니다.

14. 저도 반갑습니다.

15. 안녕하세요. 제 이름은 수지예요. (Or 저는 수지입니다.) 만나서 반갑습니다.

16. 안녕하세요. 저는 민수입니다. (Or 제 이름은 민수예요.) 만나서 반갑습니다.

17. Topic marker: 는

18. A: 안녕하세요.

19. 제 친구는 철수예요. / 제 형은 철수예요.

20. a - teacher, b - student, c - doctor

Everyday Objects
Grammar Review

This chapter focuses on how to talk about everyday objects and use basic grammar structures for describing and interacting with them.

1. Object Marker – 을/를

Used to mark the object of a verb.

- 을 is used after a consonant.

- 를 is used after a vowel.

Example: 책을 읽어요. (I read a book.) / 물을 마셔요. (I drink water.)

2. Present Tense – ~아요 / ~어요 / ~해요

Used to describe current actions or general facts.

- If the verb stem ends in ㅏ or ㅗ, use ~아요.

- If the verb stem ends in other vowels, use ~어요.

- For 하다 verbs, use ~해요.

Examples: 읽다 → 읽어요 (to read) / 가다 → 가요 (to go) / 공부하다 → 공부해요 (to study)

3. Basic Negation – 안 + Verb

Used to make negative statements.

Structure: 안 + Verb

Examples: 안 가요. (I'm not going.) / 안 먹어요. (I'm not eating.)

4. Common Everyday Vocabulary

This includes frequently used nouns such as 책 (book), 연필 (pencil), 가방 (bag), 의자 (chair), and 지우개 (eraser). These words are often combined with simple verbs like 있다 (to exist/have), 없다 (to not exist/have), 주다 (to give), and 사다 (to buy).

Mastering the object marker, basic present tense, and negation will allow learners to form essential sentences for daily communication about familiar items.

Exercises: Everyday Objects

1. Fill in the blank with the correct object marker (을/를): 연필___ 사용해요.

2. Fill in the blank with the present tense verb: 책을 (읽다) → 책을 _____.

3. Mark the object with 을/를: 저는 가방___ 샀어요.

4. Rewrite in negative form using '안': 저는 텔레비전을 봐요.

5. Match the item to the correct verb:

   a. 책   ( ) 마시다

   b. 물   ( ) 읽다

   c. 전화기   ( ) 사용하다

6. Choose the correct sentence:
   a. 저는 책을 읽어요.
   b. 저는 책이 읽어요.

7. Translate to Korean: I buy a chair.

8. Translate to Korean: I don't have a pen.

9. Correct the mistake: 저는 사과를 먹어요 안.

10. Rearrange the sentence: 연필 / 써요 / 저는

11. Write 3 sentences using the verb 있다 (to have).

12. Complete with appropriate object and verb: 저는 _____를 _____요.

13. Fill in: 저는 안 _____요. (use a verb of your choice)

14. Match the Korean nouns with their meanings:

    a. 지우개   ( ) chair

    b. 의자   ( ) eraser

    c. 가방   ( ) bag

15. Choose the appropriate verb: 저는 물을 (먹어요/마셔요).

16. Describe what you have in your bag using 2 sentences.

17. Identify the object marker in the sentence: 저는 연필을 써요.

18. Translate: I use an eraser.

19. Answer in Korean: Do you have a book? (Yes/No)

20. Write a dialogue using at least three everyday objects and two verbs.

Everyday Objects – Answer Key

1. 연필을 사용해요.

2. 책을 읽어요.

3. 저는 가방을 샀어요.

4. 저는 텔레비전을 안 봐요.

5. a-읽다, b-마시다, c-사용하다

6. a. 저는 책을 읽어요.

7. 저는 의자를 사요.

8. 저는 펜이 없어요.

9. 저는 사과를 안 먹어요.

10. 저는 연필을 써요.

11. Example answers:
   - 저는 책이 있어요.
   - 저는 펜이 있어요.

   - 저는 가방이 있어요.

12. Example answers:
   - 저는 물을 마셔요.
     - 저는 책을 읽어요.

13. Example answers:
   - 저는 안 읽어요.
   - 저는 안 마셔요.

14. a-eraser, b-chair, c-bag

15. 마셔요

16. Example:
   - 저는 가방에 연필이 있어요.
   - 지우개도 있어요.

17. Object marker: 을 (연필을)

18. 저는 지우개를 사용해요.

19. 네, 책이 있어요. / 아니요, 책이 없어요.

20. Example:
   A: 연필 있어요?
   B: 네, 연필하고 지우개가 있어요.
   A: 그럼, 책도 있어요?

Places and Possessions
Grammar Review

This chapter focuses on talking about locations, ownership, and how to construct sentences describing where something is and who it belongs to.

1. Subject Marker – 이/가

Used to indicate the subject of a sentence.

- 이 is used after a consonant.

- 가 is used after a vowel.

Example: 책이 있어요. (There is a book.) / 가방이 없어요. (There is no bag.)

2. Location Particle – 에

Used to indicate where something or someone is located.

Example: 책이 책상 위에 있어요. (The book is on the desk.)

3. Possessive Marker – 의

Used to indicate possession, equivalent to "s' in English.

Example: 민수의 가방이에요. (It's Minsu's bag.)

4. 있다 / 없다 (To have / To not have)

- 있다 is used to indicate existence or possession.

- 없다 is used to indicate non-existence or lack.

Examples: 저는 연필이 있어요. (I have a pencil.) / 저는 연필이 없어요. (I don't have a pencil.)

These grammar structures allow learners to express where things are, who owns them, and whether or not something exists.

Exercises: Places and Possessions

1. Fill in the blank with the correct subject marker (이/가): 책___ 있어요.

2. Fill in the blank with the correct location particle (에): 가방이 책상___ 있어요.

3. Use the possessive particle (의): 민수___ 연필이에요.

4. Write a sentence using 있다 to describe something you have.

5. Write a sentence using 없다 to describe something you don't have.

6. Match the item with the correct location:

    a. 책   ( ) on the desk

    b. 가방   ( ) under the table

    c. 연필   ( ) inside the bag

7. Correct the mistake: 저는 가방가 있어요.

8. Rearrange the sentence: 있어요 / 연필이 / 필통에

9. Translate into Korean: The phone is on the chair.

10. Translate into Korean: I don't have a notebook.

11. Choose the correct particle: 고양이(이/가) 의자(에/에서) 있어요.

12. Create a sentence with a person's name and something they own.

13. Describe where two items are located using 에.

14. Write a question using 있다 (e.g., Do you have a pencil?)

15. Answer the question: 책이 있어요? (Yes and No answers)

16. Fill in: 의자___ 가방이 있어요. (on the chair)

17. Complete the dialogue:

A: 볼펜이 있어요?

B: 아니요, _____.

18. Choose the correct sentence:

a. 저는 책상에 가방이 있어요.

b. 책상이 가방에 있어요.

19. Match the sentences to the translation:

a. 민수의 책이에요.   ( ) The pencil is not here.

b. 연필이 없어요.   ( ) It's Minsu's book.

c. 공책이 가방에 있어요.   ( ) The notebook is in the bag.

20. Write 3 sentences using different locations and items from your classroom or home.

Places and Possessions – Answer Key

1. 책이 있어요.

2. 가방이 책상에 있어요.

3. 민수의 연필이에요.

4. Example: 저는 지우개가 있어요.

5. Example: 저는 필통이 없어요.

6. a-책상 위에 (on the desk), b-책상 아래에 (under the desk), c-가방 안에 (inside the bag)

7. Correct: 저는 가방이 있어요.

8. 연필이 필통에 있어요.

9. 전화기가 의자 위에 있어요.

10. 저는 공책이 없어요.

11. 고양이가 의자에 있어요.

12. Example: 수지의 가방이에요.

13. Example: 책은 책상 위에 있어요. 연필은 가방 안에 있어요.

14. Example: 연필이 있어요?

15. 네, 있어요. / 아니요, 없어요.

16. 의자에 가방이 있어요.

17. 아니요, 없어요.

18. Correct: a. 저는 책상에 가방이 있어요.

19. a-It's Minsu's book., b-The pencil is not here., c-The notebook is in the bag.

20. Example:
 - 책이 책상 위에 있어요.
 - 연필이 필통 안에 있어요.
 - 가방이 의자 옆에 있어요.

Where Am I?
Grammar Review

This chapter helps learners describe their current location and ask or answer questions about where people or things are.

1. Sentence Ending – 이에요 / 예요

Used to state identity or existence in a polite and informal way.

- 이에요 is used after a consonant.

- 예요 is used after a vowel.

Example: 여기는 학교예요. (This is a school.) / 저기는 도서관이에요. (That is a library.)

2. Location Marker – 에 (at, in, on)

Used to describe the static location of someone or something.

Example: 친구가 집에 있어요. (My friend is at home.)

3. Verbs of Existence – 있다 / 없다

- 있다 indicates presence or existence.

- 없다 indicates absence or non-existence.

Examples: 고양이가 방에 있어요. (The cat is in the room.) / 선생님이 교실에 없어요. (The teacher is not in the classroom.)

4. Verbs of Motion – 가다 / 오다

- 가다 means "to go."

- 오다 means "to come."

These are frequently used with location particles to describe direction.

Examples: 학교에 가요. (I go to school.) / 집에 와요. (I come home.)

Mastering these forms helps learners describe and navigate their surroundings in Korean, both in conversation and in writing.

Exercises: Where Am I?

1. Fill in the blank with the correct form: 이것은 학교___ (이에요/예요).

2. Complete the sentence using 에: 친구가 집___ 있어요.

3. Use 있다 to write a sentence about something in your room.

4. Use 없다 to describe something not in your classroom.

5. Choose the correct form: 병원이 근처에 (있어요/가요).

6. Rearrange the sentence: 있어요 / 고양이가 / 소파에

7. Translate into Korean: The teacher is in the office.

8. Translate into Korean: The bus is not at the station.

9. Match the location with the object:

   a. 도서관   ( ) 책

   b. 식당   ( ) 음식

   c. 학교   ( ) 학생

10. Write two sentences using 가다 and 오다.

11. Use 예요/이에요 to complete: 여기는 병원＿＿.

12. Answer in Korean: Where is the cat? (Make up a location.)

13. Write a question using 어디 (Where).

14. Choose the correct verb: 저는 집에 (가요/와요).

15. Correct the mistake: 의자에 가방예요.

16. Use 있다 in a question and provide a short answer.

17. Describe where two things are using 에.

18. Identify the location marker in the sentence: 학생이 교실에 있어요.

19. Fill in the blank: 학교에 친구가 _____.

20. Write a short dialogue using two locations and three common nouns.

Where Am I? – Answer Key

1. 이것은 학교예요.

2. 친구가 집에 있어요.

3. Example: 방에 책상이 있어요.

4. Example: 교실에 텔레비전이 없어요.

5. 병원이 근처에 있어요.

6. 고양이가 소파에 있어요.

7. 선생님이 사무실에 있어요.

8. 버스가 역에 없어요.

9. a-책,   b-음식,   c-학생

10. Example: 저는 학교에 가요. 친구는 집에 와요.

11. 여기는 병원이에요.

12. Example: 고양이는 소파 위에 있어요.

13. Example: 도서관이 어디에 있어요?

14. 저는 집에 가요.

15. Corrected: 의자에 가방이 있어요.

16. Question: 펜이 있어요? Answer: 네, 있어요. / 아니요, 없어요.

17. Example: 책은 책상 위에 있어요. 연필은 가방 안에 있어요.

18. Location marker: 에

19. 학교에 친구가 있어요.

20. Example:
   A: 학교에 뭐가 있어요?
   B: 책과 연필이 있어요. 가방은 책상 옆에 있어요.

Time and Schedule
Grammar Review

This chapter focuses on how to talk about time, daily schedules, and routines using time-related vocabulary and verb forms.

1. Telling Time – 시 / 분

- 시 is used for hours, and 분 is used for minutes.

- Native Korean numbers are used for hours (한 시, 두 시, 세 시...).

- Sino-Korean numbers are used for minutes (일 분, 이 분, 삼 분...).

Example: 지금은 세 시 십오 분이에요. (It is 3:15 now.)

2. Days of the Week – 요일

- 월요일 (Monday), 화요일 (Tuesday), 수요일 (Wednesday), 목요일 (Thursday), 금요일 (Friday), 토요일 (Saturday), 일요일 (Sunday)

Example: 수요일에 수업이 있어요. (There is a class on Wednesday.)

3. Months and Dates – 월 / 일

- Sino-Korean numbers are used with 월 (month) and 일 (day).

Example: 오늘은 5 월 10 일이에요. (Today is May 10th.)

4. Present Progressive – ~고 있다
Used to describe ongoing actions.
- Attach ~고 있다 to the verb stem.

Example: 공부하고 있어요. (I am studying.)

5. Frequency and Routine Expressions
- 종종/자주 (often), 항상 (always), 가끔 (sometimes), 매일 (every day)

Example: 저는 매일 학교에 가요. (I go to school every day.)

Understanding these expressions helps learners describe what time it is, when something happens, and how frequently they do various activities.

Exercises: Time and Schedule

1. Fill in the blank: 지금은 네 ___ 십 분이에요. (시/분)

2. Match the Korean time to its English meaning:

   a. 다섯 시   ( ) 4:00

   b. 세 시 삼십 분   ( ) 5:00

   c. 네 시   ( ) 3:30

3. Translate into Korean: It is 7:15 now.

4. Write today's date in Korean (e.g., July 3rd).

5. Fill in the blank with the correct day: 오늘은 _____이에요. (Use a day of the week)

6. Fill in the correct form: 저는 지금 공부_____ 있어요.

7. Write two sentences describing your daily routine.

8. Choose the correct particle: 저는 아침에 학교(에/에서) 가요.

9. Rearrange the sentence: 있어요 / 친구하고 / 이야기하고

10. Translate into Korean: I go to the gym every Saturday.

11. Answer the question: 보통 몇 시에 일어나요? (Provide your own answer)

12. Match the day with an activity:
  a. 월요일   ( ) go shopping
  b. 수요일   ( ) go to class
  c. 토요일   ( ) go to work

13. Complete the sentence using ~고 있다: 저는 지금 책을 _____.

14. Write what you usually do on Sundays (in 2–3 sentences).

15. Identify the frequency adverb: 저는 항상 저녁에 운동해요.

16. Choose the correct response: Q: 몇 시예요? A: ( ) 열 시예요. / 안녕하세요.

17. Fill in: 저는 매일 아침 여섯 시에 _____. (verb of your choice)

18. Translate: I am reading a book now.

19. Correct the mistake: 저는 운동이 있어요.

20. Write a schedule for your school or work day (include at least 3 time-related actions).

Time and Schedule – Answer Key

1. 지금은 네 시 십 분이에요.

2. a-5:00, b-3:30, c-4:00

3. 지금은 일곱 시 십오 분이에요.

4. 오늘은 7 월 3 일이에요.

5. Example: 오늘은 화요일이에요.

6. 저는 지금 공부하고 있어요.

7. Example:
   - 아침에 일어나요.
   - 학교에 가요.

8. 저는 아침에 학교에 가요.

9. 친구하고 이야기하고 있어요.

10. 저는 매주 토요일에 헬스장에 가요.

11. Example: 저는 7 시에 일어나요.

12. a-수업에 가다 (go to class), b-일하러 가다 (go to work), c-쇼핑하다 (go shopping)

13. 저는 지금 책을 읽고 있어요.

14. Example:
   - 저는 일요일에 늦게 일어나요.
   - 보통 친구를 만나고 영화를 봐요.

15. Frequency adverb: 항상

16. 열 시예요.

17. Example: 저는 매일 아침 여섯 시에 일어나요.

18. 저는 지금 책을 읽고 있어요.

19. Corrected: 저는 운동하고 있어요.

20. Example:
   - 8 시에 아침을 먹어요.
   - 9 시에 수업을 들어요.
   - 12 시에 점심을 먹어요.

Describing People
Grammar Review

This chapter focuses on how to describe people's appearance, personality, and characteristics using basic grammar structures and descriptive vocabulary.

1. Descriptive Adjectives
- Adjectives in Korean can be used before nouns or at the end of sentences with the copula.

Example: 착한 사람 (a kind person), 그 사람은 친절해요. (That person is kind.)

2. Adjective Conjugation – ~아요 / ~어요
- Adjectives follow the same conjugation rules as verbs for present tense.

Examples: 예쁜 → 예뻐요 (pretty), 큰 → 커요 (big), 작은 → 작아요 (small)

3. Connecting Descriptions – ~고
- Use ~고 to connect multiple adjectives or actions.

Example: 그 학생은 똑똑하고 성실해요. (That student is smart and diligent.)

4. Counting People – 명 / 사람
- 명 is the counter used for people.
- Add 몇 (how many) to form questions.

Example: 몇 명이에요?/몇 명이 있어요? (How many people are there?) / 학생 두 명이 있어요. (There are two students.)

5. Honorific Nouns and Forms
- When referring to respected individuals, use honorific terms like 분 instead of 사람.

Example: 이 분은 누구세요? (Who is this person? - polite)

With these tools, learners can describe people accurately and respectfully, whether talking about physical features, traits, or counting individuals.

Exercises: Describing People

1. Fill in the blank with the correct adjective: 그 사람은 _____ (kind).

2. Conjugate the adjective into present tense: 큰 → _____.

3. Conjugate the adjective into present tense: 작은 → _____.

4. Match the adjective to its meaning:

  a. 예쁜   ( ) tall

  b. 착한   ( ) kind

  c. 키가 큰   ( ) pretty

5. Connect the two adjectives using ~고: 그는 똑똑하다 + 재미있다.

6. Rewrite using ~고: 그녀는 예쁘다. 그녀는 친절하다.

7. Use 명 to complete the sentence: 학생 세 ___이 있어요.

8. Write a question using 몇 명.

9. Translate: There are two teachers.

10. Translate: That person is tall and smart.

11. Rearrange the sentence: 있어요 / 네 명 / 학생이

12. Choose the correct honorific form: 이 사람은 / 이 분은 누구세요?

13. Describe a family member using two adjectives.

14. Identify the adjective: 그 아이는 귀여워요.

15. Fill in with an appropriate adjective: 우리 선생님은 _____해요.

16. Translate into Korean: My younger brother is short.

17. "제 친구는 아주 부드럽고 _____ 머리카락을 가지고 있어요."

a) 짧은   b) 긴

c) 작은   d) 예쁜

18. Describe your best friend in 2–3 sentences (appearance + personality).

19. Answer the question: 몇 명이 있어요? (Give a realistic answer)

20. Use the honorific form and correct the mistake: 그 사람은 예쁜 착해요.

Describing People – Answer Key

1. 그 사람은 착해요/친절해요.

2. 커요

3. 작아요

4. a-예쁜 → pretty, b-착한 → kind, c-키가 큰 → tall

5. 그는 똑똑하고 재미있어요.

6. 그녀는 예쁘고 친절해요.

7. 학생 세 명이 있어요.

8. Example: 몇 명이 있어요?

9. 선생님 두 명이 있어요.

10. 그 사람은 키가 크고 똑똑해요.

11. 학생이 네 명 있어요.

12. 이 분은 누구세요?

13. Example: 우리 아빠는 키가 크고 친절해요.

14. 귀여워요 is the adjective.

15. Example: 우리 선생님은 성실해요.

16. 제 남동생은 키가 작아요.

17. b) 긴

18. Example: 제 친구는 키가 크고 웃는 얼굴이에요. 그는 아주 친절하고 똑똑해요.

19. Example: 다섯 명이 있어요.

20. Corrected: 그 분은 예쁘고 착해요.

Making Polite Requests
Grammar Review

This chapter focuses on how to make polite requests in Korean using appropriate verb endings and expressions.

1. Polite Imperative – ~(으)세요

- Used to politely ask or tell someone to do something.

- If the verb stem ends in a consonant, use ~으세요. If it ends in a vowel, use ~세요.

Example: 앉으세요. (Please sit.) / 읽으세요. (Please read.)

2. Polite Request – ~아/어 주세요

- Used to request someone to do something for you.
- The ending attaches to the verb stem based on vowel harmony.

Examples: 도와주세요. (Please help.) / 문을 열어 주세요. (Please open the door.)

3. Offering Help or Suggestions – ~시겠어요?

- Used to politely offer or ask someone's intention.

Example: 도와주시겠어요? (Would you like to help?) / 차 한 잔 하시겠어요? (Would you like a cup of tea?)

4. Formal Nouns and Honorifics
- Use honorific expressions with elders or in formal settings.

Examples: 선생님 (teacher), 어르신 (elder), 분 (person – honorific)

These grammar patterns help learner's express requests, commands, and offers with appropriate politeness in a variety of social situations.

Exercises: Making Polite Requests

1. Conjugate into polite command form: 앉다 → _____.

2. Conjugate into polite request form: 도와주다 → _____.

3. Fill in the blank using ~(으)세요: 책을 _____. (to read)

4. Fill in the blank using ~아/어 주세요: 문을 _____. (to open)

5. Match the polite phrase with its meaning:

    a. 드시겠어요?   ( ) Would you like to drink?

    b. 앉으세요   ( ) Please sit.

    c. 도와주세요   ( ) Please help me.

6. Rewrite as a polite request: 나를 도와.

7. Rewrite using ~(으)세요: 빨리 가!

8. Write a sentence offering tea to someone (use ~시겠어요?).

9. Translate into Korean: Please close the window.

10. Translate into Korean: Would you like to eat lunch?

11. Rearrange into a polite sentence: 주세요 / 물 / 한 잔

12. Choose the correct polite form:

 a. 읽어줘요 / 읽으세요

 b. 도와줘 / 도와주세요

13. Create a short dialogue using ~아/어 주세요.

14. Write a polite request you might say to a teacher.

15. Use ~시겠어요? in a question to ask about someone's intention.

16. Fill in the blank: 도와_____. (Complete with correct polite request ending)

17. Identify the command form: 선생님, 이쪽으로 오세요.

18. Translate: Please write your name here.

19. Make a polite request involving two actions (e.g., read and return).

20. Correct the mistake: 앉으세세요.

Making Polite Requests – Answer Key

1. 앉으세요.

2. 도와주세요.

3. 책을 읽으세요.

4. 문을 열어 주세요.

5. a- Would you like to drink?, b- Please sit, c- Please help me

6. 저를 도와주세요.

7. 빨리 가세요.

8. Example: 차 한 잔 드시겠어요?

9. 창문을 닫아 주세요.

10. 점심을 드시겠어요?

11. 물 한 잔 주세요.

12. a-읽으세요, b-도와주세요

13. Example: A: 이 책을 주세요. B: 네, 여기 있어요.

14. Example: 선생님, 이 문제를 설명해 주세요.

15. Example: 지금 식사하시겠어요?

16. 도와주세요.

17. 오세요.

18. 여기에 이름을 써 주세요.

19. Example: 이 책을 읽고 돌려주세요.

20. Corrected: 앉으세요.

Asking Questions
Grammar Review

This chapter focuses on forming questions in Korean using question words and polite structures.

1. Question Words (Wh-words)

- 누구 (who), 뭐/무엇 (what), 어디 (where), 언제 (when), 왜 (why), 어떻게 (how)

Examples:

누구예요? (Who is it?)

어디에 가요? (Where are you going?)

무엇을 먹어요? (What are you eating?)

2. Sentence Endings – ~어요?/~아요?

- Used to form polite questions based on verb conjugation.

Examples: 간다 → 가요? (Are you going?) / 먹다→ 먹어요? (Are you eating?)

3. Suggestive Questions – ~(으)ㄹ까요?

- Used to make polite suggestions or ask someone's opinion.

Examples: 우리 같이 갈까요? (Shall we go together?) / 우리 무엇을/뭘 먹을까요? (What shall we eat?)

4. Yes/No Questions

- Formed using intonation or with particles.

Example: (당신은) 책을 읽어요? (Do you read books?) / 수업이 있어요? (Is there a class?)

Understanding these question patterns is essential for holding basic conversations, asking for information, and making polite suggestions.

Exercises: Asking Questions

1. Fill in the blank with the correct question word: _____에 가요? (Where are you going?)

2. Conjugate into a polite question: 먹다 → _____?

3. Rewrite as a question: 당신은 학생이에요.

4. Translate into Korean: What are you doing?

5. Match the Korean questions to their meanings:

   a. 누구예요?   ( ) What time is it?

   b. 언제 가요?   ( ) Who is it?

   c. 몇 시예요?   ( ) When are you going?

6. Use ~(으)ㄹ까요? to ask if someone wants to go eat.

7. Translate into Korean: Shall we study together?

8. Rearrange to form a proper question: 가요 / 어디에 / 지금

9. Fill in: 오늘 뭐 _____? (What are you doing today?)

10. Translate into English: 왜 학교에 가요?

11. Write a yes/no question about today's weather.

12. Create a question using 누구.

13. Identify the verb ending: 어디 가요?

14. Write a short dialogue using two questions.

15. Choose the correct question form:

  a. 먹어요 / 먹을까요?

  b. 갔어요? / 갔을텐데요?

16. Translate: How do you go to school?

17. Correct the mistake: 가요 어디에?

18. Create a polite question about someone's weekend plan.

19. Fill in with the appropriate ending: 우리 내일 영화 _____? (Shall we go to a movie?)

20. Write three questions using different wh- words.

Asking Questions – Answer Key

1. 어디에 가요?

2. 먹어요?

3. 당신은 학생이에요?

4. 뭐 해요?

5. a-누구예요? → Who is it?, b-언제 가요? → When are you going?, c-몇 시예요? → What time is it?

6. 우리 같이 먹을까요?

7. 우리 같이 공부할까요?

8. 지금 어디에 가요?

9. 오늘 뭐 해요?

10. Why are you going to school?

11. 오늘 날씨가 좋아요?

12. Example: 누구를 만났어요?

13. 요 (present polite question ending)

14. A: 어디 가요? B: 도서관에 가요. A: 누구랑 가요?

15. a-먹을까요?, b-갔어요?

16. 학교에 어떻게 가요?

17. Corrected: 어디에 가요?

18. Example: 주말에 뭐 하실 거예요?

19. 우리 내일 영화 볼까요?

20. Example:
   - 뭐 해요?
   - 어디에 가요?
   - 언제 시작해요?

Likes and Dislikes
Grammar Review

This chapter focuses on how to express likes, dislikes, and wants in Korean using common verbs and grammatical patterns.

1. 좋아하다 / 싫어하다 (to like / to dislike)

- Use object marker 을/를 before 좋아하다 or 싫어하다.

Examples: 저는 사과를 좋아해요. (I like apples.) / 그는 야채를 싫어해요. (He dislikes vegetables.)

2. ~고 싶다 (to want to...)
- Attach to verb stems to express desire.
- Conjugates like an adjective.

Examples: 먹고 싶어요. (I want to eat.) / 가고 싶어요. (I want to go.)

3. ~이/가 좋아요 / 싫어요 (to be liked / disliked)

- Use subject marker 이/가 when the item itself is liked/disliked.

Examples: 이 영화가 좋아요. (I like this movie.) / 저 음식이 싫어요. (I don't like that food.)

4. Common vocabulary for preferences
- Food, hobbies, weather, people, activities

Examples: 음악 (music), 영화 (movies), 운동 (sports), 비 (rain), 독서 (reading)

These structures help learners communicate personal preferences, feelings, and desires naturally in Korean conversation.

Exercises: Likes and Dislikes

1. Fill in the blank using 좋아하다: 저는 음악을 _____.

2. Fill in the blank using 싫어하다: 그는 야채를 _____.

3. Conjugate into ~고 싶다: 먹다 → _____.

4. Conjugate into ~고 싶다: 가다 → _____.

5. Choose the correct object marker: 저는 영화(을/를) 좋아해요.

6. Match the preference sentence with the meaning:

  a. 저는 책을 좋아해요.　　　　　　( ) I like reading books.

  b. 그는 고기를 싫어해요.　　　　　　( ) He dislikes meat.

7. Translate into Korean: I want to drink coffee.

8. Translate into Korean: I don't like cold weather.

9. Use 이/가 좋아요 to express liking for a specific thing.

10. Rearrange into a full sentence: 좋아해요 / 저는 / 운동을

11. Use ~고 싶다 in a full sentence about a weekend plan.

12. Write a sentence about something you dislike using 싫어하다.

13. Choose the correct form: 저는 지금 (먹고 싶어요 / 먹어요).

14. Write a dialogue with one person asking and another answering about a preference.

15. Translate: What do you want to do today?

16. Fill in the blank: 저는 _____을/를 좋아하지 않아요.

17. Complete the sentence using ~고 싶다: 저는 오늘 집에서 _____.

18. Match the verbs to their ~고 싶다 forms:

a. 배우다   ( ) 배우고 싶어요

b. 마시다   ( ) 마시고 싶어요

c. 자다   ( ) 자고 싶어요

19. Correct the mistake: 저는 영화를 좋아습니다.

20. Write three sentences about your likes, dislikes, and one thing you want to do.

Likes and Dislikes – Answer Key

1. 저는 음악을 좋아해요.

2. 그는 야채를 싫어해요.

3. 먹고 싶어요.

4. 가고 싶어요.

5. 를

6. a-I like reading books., b-He dislikes meat.

7. 저는 커피를 마시고 싶어요.

8. 저는 추운 날씨를 싫어해요.

9. Example: 이 음식이 좋아요.

10. 저는 운동을 좋아해요.

11. Example: 저는 주말에 영화를 보고 싶어요.

12. Example: 저는 비 오는 날을 싫어해요.

13. 먹고 싶어요.

14. Example:
   A: 음악을 좋아해요?
   B: 네, 아주 좋아해요.

15. 오늘 뭐 하고 싶어요?

16. 저는 고기를 좋아하지 않아요.

17. 저는 오늘 집에서 쉬고 싶어요.

18. a-배우고 싶어요, b-마시고 싶어요, c-자고 싶어요

19. Corrected: 저는 영화를 좋아해요.

20. Example:
   - 저는 과일을 좋아해요.
   - 저는 소음을 싫어해요.
   - 저는 여행을 가고 싶어요.

Abilities and Intentions
Grammar Review

This chapter focuses on expressing one's ability to do something and intentions using commonly used grammar patterns.

1. ~(으)ㄹ 수 있다 / ~(으)ㄹ 수 없다 (can / cannot)

- Expresses the ability or inability to do something.

- Attach to verb stem. Use ~을 after a consonant and ~ㄹ after a vowel.

Examples: 저는 수영할 수 있어요. (I can swim.) / 저는 운전할 수 없어요. (I can't drive.)

2. ~(으)려고 하다 (to intend to...)

- Used to express one's intention or plan to do something.
- Attach to the verb stem based on whether it ends in a vowel or consonant.

Examples: 저는 한국어를 배우려고 해요. (I intend to learn Korean.) / 저는 집에 가려고 해요. (I plan to go home.)

3. ~(으)ㄴ / 는 것 (nominalizing a verb)

- Turns verbs into nouns, often used with 좋아하다, 싫어하다, etc.

- ~는 것 is used for present actions, ~(으)ㄴ 것 for past actions.

Examples: 저는 요리하는 것을 좋아해요. (I like cooking.) / 읽은 책 (a book I read)

These grammar patterns help learners talk about what they can do, what they intend to do, and describe actions as concepts.

Exercises: Abilities and Intentions

1. Conjugate using ~(으)ㄹ 수 있다: 읽다 → _____.

2. Conjugate using ~(으)ㄹ 수 없다: 달리다 → _____.

3. Use ~(으)려고 하다: 저는 한국어를 배우다 → _____.

4. Fill in the blank: 저는 피아노를 칠 _____ 있어요.

5. Translate into Korean: I can cook well.

6. Translate into Korean: I can't drive.

7. Use ~(으)려고 하다 to describe your plan for today.

8. Match the sentence to its meaning:

  a. 운동하려고 해요. ( ) I can't exercise.

  b. 운동할 수 없어요. ( ) I plan to exercise.

9. Conjugate into ~는 것 form: 만들다 → _____.

10. Conjugate into ~(으)ㄴ 것 form: 듣다 (past) → _____.

11. Complete the sentence: 저는 책 읽는 것을 _____.

12. Create a sentence using both ~(으)ㄹ 수 있다 and ~(으)려고 하다.

13. Choose the correct particle: 공부할 수 (이/가) 있어요.

14. Translate into English: 저는 자전거를 탈 수 없어요.

15. Fill in: 저는 오늘 일찍 _____려고 해요.

16. Rearrange: 해요 / 수영하려고 / 저는

17. Identify the nominalized verb: 저는 노래하는 것을 좋아해요.

18. Write two sentences about something you can and cannot do.

19. Translate: I intend to travel this summer.

20. Write three sentences using one of each: 수 있다, 수 없다, ~(으)려고 하다.

Abilities and Intentions – Answer Key

1. 읽을 수 있어요.

2. 달릴 수 없어요.

3. 저는 한국어를 배우려고 해요.

4. 저는 피아노를 칠 수 있어요.

5. 저는 요리를 잘 할 수 있어요.

6. 저는 운전할 수 없어요.

7. Example: 저는 오늘 친구를 만나려고 해요.

8. a- I plan to exercise., b- I can't exercise.

9. 만드는 것

10. 들은 것

11. 저는 책 읽는 것을 좋아해요.

12. Example: 저는 수영할 수 있고 내일도 수영하려고 해요.

13. 공부할 수 있어요 (no particle needed).

14. I cannot ride a bicycle.

15. 저는 오늘 일찍 자려고 해요.

16. 저는 수영하려고 해요.

17. 노래하는 것

18. Example: 저는 노래할 수 있어요. 저는 춤출 수 없어요.

19. 저는 이번 여름에 여행하려고 해요.

20. Example:
   - 저는 운전할 수 있어요.
   - 저는 요리할 수 없어요.
   - 저는 한국어를 배우려고 해요.

Talking About the Past
Grammar Review

This chapter focuses on how to describe past events and experiences in Korean using appropriate tense markers and patterns.

1. Past Tense – ~았어요 / ~었어요 / ~했어요

- Attach to the verb stem depending on the vowel.

- Use ~았어요 after ㅏ or ㅗ; ~었어요 after other vowels; ~했어요 for 하다 verbs.

Examples: 가다 → 갔어요 (went), 먹다 → 먹었어요 (ate), 공부하다 → 공부했어요 (studied)

2. ~본 적 있다 / 없다 (have/have not tried or experienced something)

- Used to describe past experience.

- ~아/어 보다 + ~적 있다/없다

Examples: 저는 일본에 가 본 적 있어요. (I have been to Japan.) / 저는 그 영화를 본 적 없어요. (I haven't seen that movie.)

3. Time Expressions for the Past

- 어제 (yesterday), 지난주 (last week), 작년 (last year), 얼마 전에 (a while ago)

Example: 저는 어제 친구를 만났어요. (I met a friend yesterday.)

Mastering these past tense forms and expressions allows learners to talk clearly about their previous experiences and activities.

Exercises: Talking About the Past

1. Conjugate into past tense: 가다 → _____.

2. Conjugate into past tense: 먹다 → _____.

3. Conjugate into past tense: 하다 → _____.

4. Fill in the blank: 어제 친구를 _____. (to meet)

5. Translate into Korean: I studied Korean last night.

6. Translate into Korean: I didn't go to school yesterday.

7. Use ~본 적 있다: I have tried kimchi.

8. Use ~본 적 없다: I haven't watched that movie.

9. Rearrange: 봤어요 / 어제 / 영화를 / 저는

10. Fill in: 저는 일본에 _____ 적 있어요. (to go)

11. Write a sentence using 지난주 and a past activity.

12. Choose the correct tense:

  a. 공부하다 → 공부했어요 / 공부해요

  b. 보다 → 봤어요 / 봐요

13. Translate: I met my friend a while ago.

14. Identify the time expression: 지난주에 여행했어요.

15. Complete with a correct verb: 작년에 한국에서 _____.

16. Write two sentences about what you did last weekend.

17. Translate: I haven't been to Seoul.

18. Match the sentence to the meaning:

   a. 읽은 책이에요.   ( ) I read a book.

   b. 책을 읽었어요.   ( ) It's the book I read.

19. Use ~본 적 있다 in a question.

20. Write a short paragraph about a memorable experience using past tense verbs.

Talking About the Past – Answer Key

1. 갔어요

2. 먹었어요

3. 했어요

4. 저는 어제 친구를 만났어요.

5. 저는 어젯밤에 한국어를 공부했어요.

6. 저는 어제 학교에 가지 않았어요.

7. 저는 김치를 먹어 본 적 있어요.

8. 저는 그 영화를 본 적 없어요.

9. 저는 어제 영화를 봤어요.

10. 저는 일본에 간 적 있어요.

11. Example: 지난주에 친구를 만났어요.

12. a-공부했어요, b-봤어요

13. 저는 얼마 전에 친구를 만났어요.

14. Time expression: 지난주

15. 작년에 한국에서 살았어요.

16. Example: 주말에 집에서 쉬었어요. 그리고 친구를 만났어요.

17. 저는 서울에 가 본 적 없어요.

18. a-( ) It's the book I read., b-( ) I read a book.

19. Example: 김치를 먹어 본 적 있어요?

20. Example: 작년에 제주도에 갔어요. 바다를 보고 맛있는 음식을 먹었어요. 정말 재미있었어요.

Future Plans and Possibilities
Grammar Review

This chapter introduces how to talk about future plans, predictions, and possibilities in Korean using common future-related expressions.

1. ~(으)ㄹ 거예요 (will / going to)

- Used to express a future plan or prediction.

- Add ~ㄹ 거예요 to verb stems ending in vowels, and ~을 거예요 to those ending in consonants.

Examples: (저는) 갈 거예요 (I will go), (저는) 먹을 거예요 (I will eat)

2. ~(으)려고 하다 (plan/intend to)

- Used to express intention to do something (reviewed from Chapter 10).

Example: (저는) 여행을 가려고 해요. (I intend to travel.)

3. ~(으)ㄹ 것 같다 (it seems that / I think it will...)

- Used to express assumption or guess about the future.

Examples: 비가 올 것 같아요. (It looks like it will rain) / 저는 늦을 것 같아요. (I think I'll be late)

4. Time Expressions for the Future

- 내일 (tomorrow), 다음 주 (next week), 곧 (soon), 이번 주말 (this weekend)

Examples: 저는 다음 주에 시험을 볼 거예요. (I will take a test next week.)

These structures help learners discuss future events, their intentions, and their expectations with natural fluency.

Exercises: Future Plans and Possibilities

1. Conjugate using ~(으)ㄹ 거예요: 가다 → _____.

2. Conjugate using ~(으)ㄹ 거예요: 먹다 → _____.

3. Translate into Korean: I will meet my friend tomorrow.

4. Translate into Korean: I will study this weekend.

5. Fill in the blank using ~(으)려고 하다: 저는 영화를 _____.

6. Use ~(으)ㄹ 것 같다: It looks like it will rain.

7. Match the sentence to the English meaning:

  a. 갈 거예요   ( ) I think it will rain.

  b. 비가 올 것 같아요   ( ) I will go.

8. Fill in with a future time expression: 저는 _____ 여행을 갈 거예요.

9. Rearrange to make a correct sentence: 주말에 / 공부할 / 거예요 / 저는

10. Write two sentences about your plans for tomorrow.

11. Choose the correct future form:
   a. 일하다 → 일할 거예요 / 일했어요
   b. 만나다 → 만날 거예요 / 만났어요

12. Translate: I think I will be late.

13. Use ~(으)려고 하다 to describe your weekend plan.

14. Identify the future marker: 저는 운동할 거예요.

15. Complete the sentence: 비가 _____ 것 같아요.

16. Use all three structures in one paragraph (~ㄹ 거예요, ~려고 하다, ~ㄹ 것 같다).

17. Translate: I will take an exam next week.

18. Choose the right expression: (다음 주 / 지난 주)에 영화를 볼 거예요.

19. Correct the mistake: 저는 학교에 가요 거예요.

20. Write three sentences about your future plans, guesses, and intentions.

Future Plans and Possibilities – Answer Key

1. 갈 거예요.

2. 먹을 거예요.

3. 저는 내일 친구를 만날 거예요.

4. 저는 이번 주말에 공부할 거예요.

5. 보려고 해요.

6. 비가 올 것 같아요.

7. a- I will go., b- I think it will rain.

8. 다음 주에

9. 저는 주말에 공부할 거예요.

10. Example: 아침에 운동할 거예요. 오후에는 친구를 만날 거예요.

11. a-일할 거예요, b-만날 거예요

12. 저는 늦을 것 같아요.

13. Example: 저는 주말에 영화를 보려고 해요.

14. Future marker: ~ㄹ 거예요

15. 비가 올 것 같아요.

16. Example: 저는 주말에 도서관에 갈 거예요. 책을 빌리려고 해요. 날씨가 좋을 것 같아요.

17. 저는 다음 주에 시험을 볼 거예요.

18. 다음 주

19. Corrected: 저는 학교에 갈 거예요.

20. Example: 저는 다음 주에 여행할 거예요. 날씨가 좋을 것 같아요. 친구를 만나려고 해요.

Daily Routines
Grammar Review

This chapter focuses on vocabulary and grammar for describing regular habits and daily routines in Korean.

1. Present Tense ~아요 / ~어요 / ~해요

- Used for expressing regular or habitual actions.

- ~아요 for stems ending in ㅏ or ㅗ, ~어요 for others, ~해요 for 하다 verbs.

Examples: 일어나다 → 일어나요 (wake up), 먹다 → 먹어요 (eat), 공부하다 → 공부해요 (study)

2. Time Expressions of Routine

- 매일 (every day), 아침에 (in the morning), 점심에 (at lunchtime), 저녁에 (in the evening), 밤에 (at night)

Examples: 저는 매일 아침에 운동해요. (I exercise every morning.)

3. Sequence Words – 그리고 / 그다음에 / 먼저

- Used to describe the order of daily activities.

Examples: 먼저 저는 일어나요. 그리고 (저는) 세수해요. (First I wake up. Then I wash my face.)

4. Frequency Adverbs – 자주, 항상, 가끔, 거의, 전혀

- Used to indicate how often you do something.

Examples: 저는 자주 커피를 마셔요. (I often drink coffee.) / 저는 전혀 운동을 하지 않아요. (I never exercise.)

Understanding these grammar rules helps learners clearly describe how their day usually goes, making conversations more fluent and personal.

Exercises: Daily Routines

1. Conjugate into present tense: 일어나다 → _____.

2. Conjugate into present tense: 먹다 → _____.

3. Translate into Korean: I study Korean every evening.

4. Translate into Korean: I exercise in the morning.

5. Fill in the blank with a frequency adverb: 저는 _____ 커피를 마셔요. (often)

6. Match the time expression with the meaning:

   a. 아침에   ( ) at night

   b. 점심에   ( ) in the morning

   c. 밤에   ( ) at lunchtime

7. Use 그리고 to connect two actions about your day.

8. Rearrange: 매일 / 저는 / 학교에 / 가요

9. Fill in: 저는 매일 아침에 _____요. (wake up)

10. Write two sentences using 자주 and 전혀.

11. Use 그다음에 in a sentence describing your routine.

12. Complete with a sequence word: 저는 아침을 먹어요. _____ 이를 닦아요.

13. Choose the correct conjugation to express regular or habitual actions:
 a. 가다 → 가요 / 갔어요
 b. 하다 → 해요 / 했어요

14. Identify the adverb: 저는 항상 늦게 자요.

15. Translate: I go to bed late every night.

16. Describe your morning routine using at least 3 verbs.

17. Use 먼저 in a sentence about your daily start.

18. Translate: I don't usually eat breakfast.

19. Write a short paragraph about your daily routine.

20. Correct the mistake: 저는 저녁에 숙제를 해요. 그리고 잔다.

Daily Routines – Answer Key

1. 일어나요.　　　　　　　　　　　　2. 먹어요.

3. 저는 매일 저녁에 한국어를 공부해요.

4. 저는 아침에 운동해요.　　　　　　5. 자주

6. a- in the morning, b- at lunchtime, c- at night

7. Example: 저는 아침에 일어나요. 그리고 운동해요.

8. 저는 매일 학교에 가요.　　　　　　9. 일어나요

10. Example: 저는 물을 자주 마셔요. 저는 전혀 무섭지 않아요.

11. Example: 저는 세수해요. 그다음에 옷을 입어요.

12. 그리고

13. a-가요, b-해요

14. 항상

15. 저는 매일 밤 늦게 자요.

16. Example: 저는 일어나요. 세수해요. 아침을 먹어요.

17. Example: 먼저 알람을 끄고 일어나요.

18. 저는 보통 아침을 안 먹어요.

19. Example: 저는 매일 아침 7시에 일어나요. 그리고 세수하고 아침을 먹어요. 학교에 가고 저녁에는 공부해요.

20. Corrected: 저는 저녁에 숙제를 해요. 그리고 자요.

Making Plans with Others
Grammar Review

This chapter focuses on the grammar and expressions needed to make plans with others and respond to invitations politely.

1. ~(으)ㄹ래요? (Shall we...? / Would you like to...?)

- Used to suggest an activity or ask about someone's intention informally.

- Attach ~ㄹ래요 after vowel-ending stems and ~을래요 after consonant-ending stems.

Examples: 같이 영화 볼래요? (Shall we watch a movie together?) / 뭐 먹을래요? (What would you like to eat?)

2. ~고 싶다 vs. ~(으)ㄹ래요

- ~고 싶다 expresses personal desire, while ~(으)ㄹ래요 is used to invite or suggest.

Examples: 저는 쉬고 싶어요. (I want to rest.) / 쉬고 싶으세요? (Do you want to rest?)

3. ~(으)ㅂ시다 (Let's... – formal)

- Used to formally suggest doing something together.

Examples: 식사합시다. (Let's eat.) / 같이 갑시다. (Let's go together.)

4. Responding to Invitations

- 좋아요 (Sounds good), 네, 괜찮아요 (Sure, that's fine), 미안해요 (Sorry), 다음에요 (Maybe next time)

Example: A: 같이 점심 먹을래요? B: 미안해요. 다음에요.

These expressions are essential for setting up social interactions and making polite arrangements with friends, classmates, and colleagues.

Exercises: Making Plans with Others

1. Conjugate using ~(으)ㄹ래요?: 보다 → _____.

2. Conjugate using ~(으)ㄹ래요?: 먹다 → _____.

3. Translate into Korean: Shall we drink coffee together?

4. Translate into Korean: What would you like to do this weekend?

5. Fill in the blank with ~(으)ㄹ래요: 같이 점심을 _____?

6. Choose the correct form for making a suggestion:

 a. 갈래요? / 갔어요?

 b. 먹을래요? / 먹었어요?

7. Use ~고 싶다 in a sentence about your own desire.

8. Use ~(으)ㄹ래요? in a sentence to make a suggestion.

9. Conjugate formally using ~(으)ㅂ시다: 공부하다 → _____.

10. Translate: Let's go shopping.

11. Rearrange: 저는 / 같이 / 영화 / 보고 / 싶어요

12. Fill in with an appropriate response: A: 내일 같이 점심 먹을래요? B: _____.

13. Use 다음에요 in a polite refusal.

14. Write a dialogue using ~(으)ㄹ래요? and a polite response.

15. Translate: I want to rest at home.

16. Complete the invitation: 우리 같이 _____? (to watch a movie)

17. Identify the suggestion form: 우리 공원에 갈래요?

18. Write two questions using ~(으)ㄹ래요.

19. Choose the right verb ending: (갑시다 / 갈 거예요) when making a formal plan.

20. Write a short paragraph describing a plan you want to make with a friend.

Making Plans with Others – Answer Key

1. 볼래요?

2. 먹을래요?

3. 같이 커피 마실래요?

4. 이번 주말에 뭐 할래요?

5. 먹을래요?

6. a-갈래요?, b-먹을래요?

7. Example: 저는 집에서 쉬고 싶어요.

8. Example: 같이 영화 볼래요?

9. 공부합시다.

10. 쇼핑하러 갑시다.

11. 저는 같이 영화 보고 싶어요.

12. 좋아요.

13. 미안해요. 다음에요.

14. A: 같이 점심 먹을래요?

    B: 네, 좋아요.

15. 저는 집에서 쉬고 싶어요.

16. 영화 볼래요?

17. ~(으)ㄹ래요

18. Example: 같이 저녁 먹을래요? / 영화 볼래요?

19. 갑시다

20. Example: 다음 주에 친구와 함께 등산을 하려고 해요. 먼저 아침을 먹고, 산에 갈 거예요. 점심은 같이 먹을래요.

At a Restaurant
Grammar Review

This chapter covers key expressions and grammar for ordering food, asking for help, and interacting in a restaurant setting.

1. ~(으)세요 (Please do... – polite request)

- Used to politely ask for an action.

Examples: 주문하세요. (Please order.) / 앉으세요. (Please sit.)

2. ~고 싶어요 (I want to...)

- Used to express desire, especially when ordering.

Example: 김밥을 먹고 싶어요. (I want to eat gimbap.)

3. ~(으)로 주세요 (Please give me...)

- Used for requesting items.

Examples: 물로 주세요. (Water, please.) / 이걸로 주세요. (Please give me this one.)

4. Counters – 개, 잔, 병, 그릇

- Used to count food and drinks.

Examples: 물 두 잔 주세요. (Two glasses of water, please.) / 김치찌개 한 그릇 주세요. (One bowl of kimchi stew, please.)

5. Making polite requests with 주세요 and honorifics

- Common for ordering or asking a favor politely.

Examples: 메뉴 좀 주세요. (Please give me the menu.) / 계산서 주세요. (Check, please.)

These patterns help learners navigate menus, order food, and communicate clearly and politely in restaurants.

Exercises: At a Restaurant

1. Conjugate into polite request: 주문하다 → _____.

2. Conjugate into ~고 싶어요: 먹다 → _____.

3. Translate: I want to eat bulgogi.

4. Translate: Please give me two bowls of rice.

5. Fill in the blank: 물 한 _____ 주세요. (Use the correct counter)

6. Match the request with the item:

   a. 계산서 주세요   ( ) menu

   b. 메뉴 주세요   ( ) bill/check

   c. 물 주세요   ( ) water

7. Rearrange: 주세요 / 이걸 / 로

8. Fill in the blank with ~(으)세요: 자리에 _____.

9. Use ~고 싶어요 in a full sentence about ordering food.

10. Create a dialogue between a customer and server including at least two polite requests.

11. Translate: One bottle of soju, please.

12. Fill in: 김밥 한 _____ 주세요. (Use the correct counter)

13. Choose the correct polite form:
   a. 드세요 / 먹어요
   b. 주세요 / 줘요

14. Identify the honorific: 이쪽으로 앉으세요.

15. Translate: May I have the menu, please?

16. Write a short list of 3 food or drink orders with correct counters and polite forms.

17. Use '~로 주세요' to order using a pointing expression.

18. Translate: I want to try tteokbokki.

19. Correct the mistake: 물 한 병 싶어요.

20. Write a paragraph describing how you would order a meal at a restaurant in Korean.

At a Restaurant – Answer Key

1. 주문하세요.

2. 먹고 싶어요.

3. 저는 불고기를 먹고 싶어요.

4. 밥 두 그릇 주세요.

5. 잔

6. a- bill/check, b- menu, c- water

7. 이걸로 주세요.

8. 자리에 앉으세요.

9. Example: 저는 김치찌개를 먹고 싶어요.

10. Example:

   A: 메뉴 좀 주세요.

   B: 네, 여기 있습니다.

   A: 김밥 한 줄 주세요.

   B: 알겠습니다.

11. 소주 한 병 주세요.

12. 줄

13. a-드세요, b-주세요

14. Honorific: 앉으세요

15. 메뉴 좀 주세요.

16. Example:

   - 물 두 잔 주세요.

   - 김밥 한 줄 주세요.

   - 된장찌개 한 그릇 주세요.

17. Example: 이걸로 주세요.

18. 저는 떡볶이를 먹어 보고 싶어요.

19. Corrected: 물 한 병 주세요 / 물을 마시고 싶어요.

20. Example: 식당에 가면 먼저 자리에 앉고 메뉴를 봐요. 김밥 한 줄과 물 한 잔을 주문하고 계산서도 부탁해요.

Shopping and Money
Grammar Review

This chapter covers useful grammar and expressions for shopping, asking about prices, and handling money in Korean.

1. 얼마예요? (How much is it?)

- The basic expression to ask about price.

Example: 이거 얼마예요? (How much is this?)

2. Sino-Korean Numbers for Money

- Use 일, 이, 삼, 사... with units like 백 (hundred), 천 (thousand), 만 (ten thousand)

- Currency: 원 (won).

Examples: 오천 원 (5,000 won), 만오천 원 (15,000 won)

3. ~하고 / ~(이)랑 (and / with)

- Used to list or connect nouns.

Examples: 사과하고 바나나 주세요. (Please give me an apple and a banana.)

4. ~좀 주세요 / 좀 깎아 주세요 (Please give me... / Please give me a discount)

- Polite request forms used frequently in markets and stores.

Examples: 이거 좀 주세요. (Please give me this one.) / 좀 깎아 주세요. (Please give me a discount.)

5. ~밖에 + Negative (only, nothing but)

- Used to express limitation with a negative verb.

Examples: 천 원밖에 없어요. (I only have 1,000 won.) / 돈이 조금밖에 없어요. (I have only a little money.)

These grammar forms are helpful for navigating shopping scenarios, negotiating prices, and discussing how much something costs.

Exercises: Shopping and Money

1. Translate into Korean: How much is this?

2. Write the following amount in Korean: 7,000 won

3. Write the following amount in Korean: 18,500 won

4. Use ~하고 in a sentence listing two items you want to buy.

5. Translate: Please give me this and that.

6. Use Sino-Korean numbers to complete: 사과는 _____ 원이에요.

7. Fill in the blank with ~좀 주세요: 이 책을 _____.

8. Fill in the blank with a polite discount request: _____ 주세요. (Ask for a discount)

9. Translate: I only have 5,000 won.

10. Rearrange to form a polite request: 주세요 / 이거 / 좀

11. Choose the correct particle: 바나나(하고/에서) 우유

12. Match the Korean phrase with the English meaning:

   a. 깎아 주세요   ( ) This one, please

   b. 이거 주세요   ( ) Please give me a discount

13. Translate: Please give me one apple and two bananas.

14. Complete using 밖에: 돈이 조금_____.

15. Translate: I have nothing but 1,000 won.

16. Use ~(이)랑 in a shopping sentence.

17. Create a dialogue asking for the price of an item and requesting it politely.

18. Identify the use of Sino-Korean number: 오천 원

19. Correct the mistake: 만 원 있어요 밖에.

20. Write a paragraph about buying food at a market using at least 3 grammar forms from this chapter.

Shopping and Money – Answer Key

1. 이거 얼마예요?

2. 칠천 원

3. 만 팔천 오백 원

4. 사과하고 바나나를 사고 싶어요.

5. 이거하고 저거 주세요.

6. Example: 사과는 삼천 원이에요.

7. 이 책을 좀 주세요.

8. 좀 깎아 주세요.

9. 저는 오천 원밖에 없어요.

10. 이거 좀 주세요.

11. 바나나하고 우유

12. a- Please give me a discount, b- This, please

13. 사과 한 개하고 바나나 두 개 주세요.

14. 밖에 없어요.

15. 저는 천 원밖에 없어요.

16. Example: 우유랑 빵을 샀어요. (or 빵이랑 우유를 샀어요.)

17. Example:
   A: 이거 얼마예요?
   B: 오천 원이에요.
   A: 이거 좀 주세요.

18. 오천 원 = 5,000 won (uses Sino-Korean numbers)

19. Corrected: 만 원밖에 없어요.

20. Example: 시장에서 사과하고 배를 샀어요. 사과는 삼천 원, 배는 오천 원이었어요.
"이거 좀 주세요"하고 "깎아 주세요"도 말했어요. 돈이 만 원밖에 없었어요.

At the Doctor's Office
Grammar Review

This chapter focuses on grammar and expressions used to describe symptoms, ask for help, and understand instructions at a doctor's office.

1. ~이/가 아파요 (It hurts / I am sick)

- Used to describe pain or discomfort.

Examples: 저는 머리가 아파요. (I have a headache.) / 저는 배가 아파요. (My stomach hurts.)

2. ~았/었어요 for Past Medical Symptoms

- Used to describe symptoms that have already occurred.

Examples: 저는 어제 열이 있었어요. (I had a fever yesterday.) / 저는 기침을 했어요. (I coughed.)

3. ~(으)면 (if/when)

- Used to describe a condition or possibility.

Examples: 아프면 병원에 가세요. (If you are sick, go see a doctor.) / 시간이 있으면 저는 약국에 가요. (If I have time, I go to the pharmacy.)

4. ~지 마세요 (Please don't...)

- Used for giving negative instructions politely.

Examples: 걱정하지 마세요. (Don't worry.) / 무리하지 마세요. (Don't overdo it.)

These grammar points help learners explain health problems, respond to doctors, and follow or give simple instructions in a medical setting.

Exercises: At the Doctor's Office

1. Translate: My head hurts.

2. Translate: I had a fever yesterday.

3. Fill in the blank using ~이/가 아파요: 저는 _____가 아파요. (Use a body part)

4. Use ~았/었어요 to describe a past symptom.

5. Rearrange: 아파요 / 배가 / 지금

6. Use ~(으)면 in a sentence about going to see a doctor.

7. Translate: If you are sick, take medicine.

8. Use ~지 마세요 in a sentence telling someone not to worry.

9. Complete the sentence with ~지 마세요: 운동을 _____.

10. Translate: I had a cold last week.

11. Choose the correct form (past):

   a. 기침하다 → 기침했어요 / 기침해요

   b. 열이 있다 → 열이 있었어요 / 열이 있어요

12. Identify the conditional: 아프면 병원에 가세요.

13. Write a short dialogue between a patient and doctor including symptoms and advice.

14. Translate: Please don't overdo it.

15. Fill in the blank using ~(으)면: 시간이 _____ 약국에 가요.

16. Translate: My stomach hurts, so I'm going to see a doctor.

17. Use ~았/었어요 in a sentence about a symptom you experienced.

18. Complete: 어제 머리가 아파서 _____.

19. Correct the mistake: 기침하지 마해요.

20. Write a paragraph describing a visit to the doctor using at least 3 grammar points from this chapter.

At the Doctor's Office – Answer Key

1. 저는 머리가 아파요.

2. 저는 어제 열이 있었어요.

3. Example: 저는 배가 아파요.

4. Example: 어제 기침을 했어요.

5. 지금 배가 아파요.

6. Example: 아프면 병원에 가요.

7. 아프면 약을 드세요.

8. 걱정하지 마세요.

9. 운동을 하지 마세요.

10. 지난주에 감기에 걸렸어요.

11. a-기침했어요, b-열이 있었어요

12. Conditional: 아프면

13. Example:

   A: 어디가 아파요?

   B: 머리가 아파요.

   A: 약을 드세요. 무리하지 마세요.

14. 무리하지 마세요.

15. 있으면

16. 배가 아파서 병원에 가요.

17. Example: 저는 어제 열이 있었어요.

18. 병원에 갔어요.

19. Corrected: 기침하지 마세요.

20. Example: 어제 배가 아팠어요. 병원에 갔고 의사 선생님이 약을 주셨어요. 무리하지 말라고 했어요.

Giving and Receiving
Grammar Review

This chapter covers how to express giving and receiving actions in Korean, including honorific and casual forms.

1. 주다 / 드리다 (to give)

- 주다 is used casually, 드리다 is the honorific form.

Examples: 저는 선물을 줬어요. (I gave a gift.) / 저는 그것을 선생님께 드렸어요. (I gave it to the teacher.)

2. 받다 (to receive)

- Used for receiving something from someone.

Examples: 저는 친구에게 편지를 받았어요. (I received a letter from a friend.)

3. ~에게 / ~께 (to someone)

- ~에게 is the standard form; ~께 is the honorific form.

Examples: 저는 부모님께 선물을 드렸어요. (I gave a gift to my parents.) / 저는 친구에게 책을 줬어요. (I gave a book to a friend.)

4. Noun + 을/를 + 주다/받다/드리다

- Combine the object with the verb for clarity.

Examples: 꽃을 줬어요. (Gave flowers) / 책을 받았어요. (Received a book)

5. ~한테서 / ~에게서 (from someone)

- Used to indicate from whom something is received.

Examples: 친구한테서 선물을 받았어요. (Received a gift from a friend.)

These grammar points help learners clearly explain acts of giving and receiving in social and formal contexts.

Exercises: Giving and Receiving

1. Conjugate 주다 in past tense: _____.

2. Conjugate 받다 in past tense: _____.

3. Translate: I gave a gift to my teacher.

4. Translate: I received a letter from my friend.

5. Fill in the blank with ~에게 or ~께: 선생님___ 드렸어요.

6. Match the phrase with its meaning:

   a. 책을 받았어요   ( ) I gave a book

   b. 책을 드렸어요   ( ) I received a book

7. Complete: 저는 부모님___ 꽃을 드렸어요. (honorific)

8. Use ~한테서 in a sentence about receiving something.

9. Translate: I gave a pen to my classmate.

10. Rearrange: 받았어요 / 선물을 / 친구에게서

11. Use 주다 in a sentence with a specific noun.

12. Use 드리다 in a polite sentence involving a teacher.

13. Fill in: 저는 친구에게 이메일을 _____.

14. Choose the correct honorific:

a. 부모님에게 / 부모님께

b. 선생님에게 / 선생님께

15. Translate: I received a present from my mom.

16. Complete the sentence using 을/를 and 주다: 사과 ___ 동생에게 ____.

17. Identify the recipient particle in the sentence: 친구에게 선물을 줬어요.

18. Correct the mistake: 저는 선생님에게 드렸어요.

19. Use both 주다 and 받다 in a short sentence.

20. Write a paragraph describing a time you gave and received gifts, using at least three grammar patterns from this chapter.

Giving and Receiving – Answer Key

1. 줬어요

2. 받았어요

3. 저는 선생님께 선물을 드렸어요.

4. 저는 친구에게서 편지를 받았어요.

5. 께

6. a- I received a book, b- I gave a book

7. 께

8. Example: 친구한테서 책을 받았어요.

9. 저는 반친구에게 펜을 줬어요.

10. 친구에게서 선물을 받았어요.

11. Example: 저는 동생에게 사과를 줬어요.

12. Example: 선생님께 편지를 드렸어요.

13. 받았어요.

14. a-부모님께, b-선생님께

15. 저는 엄마에게 선물을 받았어요.

16. 사과를 동생에게 줬어요.

17. 에게

18. Corrected: 저는 선생님께 드렸어요.

19. Example: 저는 친구에게 선물을 줬고 친구한테서 편지를 받았어요.

20. Example: 지난 생일에 친구에게 선물을 줬어요. 친구한테서 케이크를 받았어요.
선생님께도 꽃을 드렸어요.

Transportation and Directions
Grammar Review

This chapter introduces grammar and vocabulary for giving and understanding directions, and talking about transportation in Korean.

1. ~(으)로 (to/toward/by means of)

- Indicates direction or means of transportation.

Examples: 지하철로 가요. (I go by subway.) / 오른쪽으로 가세요. (Go to the right.)

2. ~에 가다 / ~에서 오다 (to go to / to come from)

- Used with places to indicate direction of travel.

Examples: 학교에 가요. (I go to school.) / 집에서 왔어요. (I came from home.)

3. ~까지 / ~부터 (until / from)

- Used to show range or start and end points.

Examples: 서울부터 부산까지 (from Seoul to Busan), 집에서 학교까지 (from home to school)

4. Directional Verbs – 가다, 오다, 타다, 내리다, 갈아타다

- Useful for giving and following directions.

Examples: 저는 버스를 타요. (I take the bus.) / 다음 역에서 내리세요. (Please get off at the next station.)

5. ~는 길이에요 (I'm on my way...)

- Used to describe one's current travel or path.

Example: 지금 가는 길이에요. (I'm on my way now.)

These grammar forms allow learners to confidently navigate, describe travel routes, and ask for or give directions in real-life situations.

Exercises: Transportation and Directions

1. Translate: I go by subway.

2. Translate: Please go to the right.

3. Fill in the blank: 학교___ 가요. (to)

4. Translate: I came from home.

5. Use ~까지 to say: from home to school.

6. Use ~부터 and ~까지 in a sentence.

7. Match the transportation verb with its meaning:

  a. 타다   ( ) to get off

  b. 내리다   ( ) to ride

8. Fill in: 지금 _____ 길이에요. (on the way)

9. Use ~(으)로 with a mode of transport.

10. Rearrange: 서울 / 부산 / 가요 / 에서 / 에

11. Translate: Please get off at the next station.

12. Use 갈아타다 in a sentence.

13. Fill in with the correct verb: 버스를 _____요. (to ride)

14. Write a dialogue asking how to get to the subway station.

15. Identify the directional phrase: 집에서 학교까지

16. Translate: I go to work by bus.

17. Use ~는 길이에요 to describe going somewhere now.

18. Correct the mistake: 저는 집에 왔어요에서.

19. Translate: I transferred at Gangnam Station.

20. Write a paragraph describing how you go from home to school/work using at least three grammar points from this chapter.

Transportation and Directions – Answer Key

1. 저는 지하철로 가요.

2. 오른쪽으로 가세요.

3. 에

4. 집에서 왔어요.

5. 집에서 학교까지

6. Example: 서울부터 부산까지 기차를 탔어요.

7. a- to ride, b- to get off

8. 가는

9. Example: 택시로 갔어요.

10. 서울에서 부산에 가요.

11. 다음 역에서 내리세요.

12. Example: 강남역에서 2호선으로 갈아탔어요.

13. 버스를 타요 (or 버스를 탔어요)

14. Example:
   A: 지하철역에 어떻게 가요?
   B: 버스로 가세요.

15. 에서, 까지

16. 저는 버스로 출근해요.

17. Example: 지금 학교에 가는 길이에요.

18. Corrected: 저는 집에서 왔어요.

19. 저는 강남역에서 갈아탔어요.

20. Example: 저는 집에서 학교까지 버스로 가요. 먼저 버스를 타고 다음 정류장에서 갈아타요. 지금 가는 길이에요.

Weather and Seasons
Grammar Review

This chapter introduces vocabulary and grammar related to weather and seasons, helping learners describe the environment and talk about the time of year.

1. ~네요 (expressing realization or surprise)
- Often used to comment on the weather.
Examples: 날씨가 좋네요! (The weather is nice!) / 많이 춥네요! (It's really cold!)

2. ~지만 (but / although)
- Used to contrast two clauses.
Examples: 날씨는 춥지만, 좋아해요. (It's cold, but I like it.) / 비가 오지만 산책해요. (It's raining, but I go for a walk.)

3. Weather Verbs – 비가 오다, 눈이 오다, 바람이 불다, 해가 나다
- Common expressions to describe weather.
Examples: 비가 와요. (It's raining.) / 바람이 불어요. (It's windy.)

4. Seasonal Vocabulary – 봄 (spring), 여름 (summer), 가을 (fall/autumn), 겨울 (winter)
Examples: 봄에는 꽃이 피어요. (Flowers bloom in spring.) / 겨울에 눈이 많이 와요. (It snows a lot in winter.)

5. Temperature Expressions – 덥다, 춥다, 따뜻하다, 시원하다
Examples: 오늘은 덥네요. (It's hot today.) / 가을 날씨는 시원해요. (Fall weather is cool.)

These grammar forms are useful for everyday conversations about the weather, planning seasonal activities, and reacting to current conditions.

Exercises: Weather and Seasons

1. Translate: The weather is nice! (express surprise)

2. Translate: It's cold, but I like it.

3. Fill in the blank with ~네요: 오늘은 정말 _____. (덥다)

4. Use ~지만 to contrast two weather ideas.

5. Use ~네요 in a sentence about the wind.

6. Identify the weather verb: 비가 와요.

7. Match the season with the description:

   a. 봄   ( ) It snows a lot.

   b. 여름   ( ) Flowers bloom.

   c. 겨울   ( ) It's hot.

8. Translate: It snows a lot in winter.

9. Use a temperature adjective in a sentence about today.

10. Translate: Although it's raining, I'm going for a walk.

11. Fill in: 가을에는 날씨가 _____. (cool)

12. Use ~지만 in a sentence about summer.

13. Rearrange: 눈이 / 겨울에 / 많이 / 와요

14. Identify the expression of surprise: 날씨가 좋네요.

15. Translate: It's really windy today! (use ~네요)

16. Write a sentence using two weather verbs.

17. Translate: Spring is warm and flowers bloom.

18. Use a seasonal noun and weather verb in a sentence.

19. Correct the mistake: 비가 와지만 추워요.

20. Write a paragraph describing the four seasons in Korea using vocabulary and grammar from this chapter.

Weather and Seasons – Answer Key

1. 날씨가 좋네요!

2. 날씨는 춥지만, 좋아해요.

3. 덥네요.

4. Example: 비가 오지만 날씨가 시원해요.

5. 바람이 많이 부네요.

6. Verb: 오다 (in 비가 오다)

7. a- Flowers bloom, b- It's hot, c- It snows a lot

8. 겨울에 눈이 많이 와요.

9. 오늘은 덥고 햇빛이 강해요.

10. 비가 오지만 산책해요.

11. 시원해요.

12. Example: 여름은 덥지만 재미있어요.

13. 겨울에 눈이 많이 와요.

14. 네요

15. 오늘은 정말 바람이 많이 부네요!

16. Example: 비가 오고 바람이 불어요.

17. 봄은 따뜻하고 꽃이 피어요.

18. Example: 여름에는 비가 자주 와요.

19. Corrected: 비가 오지만 추워요.

20. Example: 한국에는 봄, 여름, 가을, 겨울이 있어요. 봄에는 꽃이 피고 따뜻해요. 여름에는 덥고 비가 와요. 가을에는 시원하고 하늘이 맑아요. 겨울에는 눈이 많이 와요.

Shopping and Bargaining
Grammar Review

This chapter builds on shopping and money language with a focus on counting units, making polite requests, expressing preferences, and bargaining.

1. Counting Units (개, 병, 장, 권, 벌, 대, 켤레, 마리, 송이, etc.)
- Used with Sino-Korean or native Korean numbers depending on context.
Examples: 사과 두 개 (two apples), 책 한 권 (one book), 신발 한 켤레 (a pair of shoes)

2. Numbers
- Sino-Korean numbers: 일, 이, 삼... (used with money, dates, phone numbers, etc.)
- Native Korean numbers: 하나 (or 한), 둘 (or 두), 셋... (used with general counting, age, hours, etc.)

3. ~고 싶다 (I want to...)
- Used to express preference.
Example: 이 옷을 사고 싶어요. (I want to buy these clothes.)

4. ~좀 깎아 주세요 (Please give me a discount)
- A polite way to request a lower price when shopping.
Example: 이거 좀 깎아 주세요. (Please give me a discount on this.)

These grammar patterns allow learners to confidently engage in shopping conversations, express what they want, count items correctly, and ask for discounts politely.

Exercises: Shopping and Bargaining

1. Translate: I want to buy three apples.

2. Use a native Korean number and counter to say 'five bottles of water'.

3. Translate: Please give me a discount on this.

4. Use ~고 싶다 in a sentence about shopping.

5. Fill in the blank: 이 신발 한 _____ 주세요. (counter for shoes)

6. Write a sentence using the counter '권' (for books).

7. Translate: I want to buy two t-shirts.

8. Match the number with the correct item:

   a. 두 병   ( ) books

   b. 세 권   ( ) bottles

   c. 한 켤레   ( ) shoes

9. Complete: 저는 이 가방을 _____ 싶어요.

10. Rearrange: 주세요 / 좀 / 이거 / 깎아

11. Choose the correct counter: 장 / 개 / 권 for a notebook

12. Use a Sino-Korean number to say the price: 15,000 won

13. Fill in: 사과 _____ 개 주세요.

14. Use a shopping verb and ~고 싶다 together in a sentence.

15. Translate: Please give me a discount. I want to buy two.

16. Identify the use of a native Korean number: 바나나 세 개 주세요.

17. Write a mini dialogue between a buyer and seller involving numbers and bargaining.

18. Use at least two different counters in one sentence.

19. Correct the mistake: 저는 두 책을 사고 싶어요.

20. Write a paragraph about a market shopping experience using counters, numbers, and ~고 싶다.

Shopping and Bargaining – Answer Key

1. 사과를 세 개 사고 싶어요.

2. 물 다섯 병

3. 이거 좀 깎아 주세요.

4. Example: 이 치마를 사고 싶어요.

5. 켤레

6. Example: 저는 책 두 권을 샀어요.

7. 저는 티셔츠를 두 벌 사고 싶어요.

8. a- bottles, b- books, c- shoes

9. 사고

10. 이거 좀 깎아 주세요.

11. 권

12. 만오천 원

13. 세

14. Example: 저는 바지를 사고 싶어요.

15. 좀 깎아 주세요. 두 개 사고 싶어요.

16. Native Korean: 세

17. Example:

A: 이 가방 얼마예요?

B: 이만 원이에요.

A: 좀 깎아 주세요. 두 개 사고 싶어요.

B: 알겠습니다. 만팔천 원이에요.

18. Example: 사과 세 개하고 우유 두 병 주세요.

19. Corrected: 책을 두 권 사고 싶어요.

20. Example: 시장에 가서 사과 세 개, 바나나 두 송이, 우유 한 병을 샀어요. 과일을 더 사고 싶었지만 돈이 없어서 깎아 달라고 했어요.

Making Plans with Friends
Grammar Review

This chapter introduces key grammar patterns for making plans, extending invitations, and deciding on actions with friends.

1. ~(으)ㄹ까요? (Shall we...? / Do you want to...?)
- Used to suggest doing something together or to ask what someone thinks.
Examples: 우리 무엇을/뭘 먹을까요? (What shall we eat?) / 같이 영화 볼까요? (Shall we watch a movie together?)

2. ~는데 / ~은데 (Setting background or contrast)
- Used to provide background information or contrast before a suggestion or invitation.
Examples: 지금 바쁜데 나중에 만날까요? (I'm busy now, shall we meet later?) / 오늘은 날씨가 좋은데 산책할까요? (The weather is nice today, shall we take a walk?)

3. ~기로 하다 (Decided to...)
- Used to express a decision to do something.
Examples: 저는 친구를 만나기로 했어요. (I decided to meet my friend.) / 우리는 여행을 가기로 했어요. (We decided to go on a trip.)

These grammar patterns help learners invite others, express decisions, and structure plans naturally in conversational Korean.

Exercises: Making Plans with Friends

1. Translate: Shall we go to the park?

2. Translate: I decided to call my friend.

3. Fill in the blank using ~(으)ㄹ까요?: 영화 _____까요? (보다)

4. Use ~기로 하다 in a sentence about making weekend plans.

5. Translate: I'm tired, but shall we take a walk? (use ~은데/~는데 and ~(으)ㄹ까요?)

6. Rearrange to form a correct sentence: 친구를 / 했어요 / 만나기로 / 저는

7. Use ~는데 in a sentence setting up an invitation.

8. Complete with ~(으)ㄹ까요?: 우리 내일 뭐 _____?

9. Translate: The weather is nice, shall we ride bikes?

10. Fill in: 낮에는 바쁜데 _____에 만날까요?

11. Use all three forms (~는데, ~(으)ㄹ까요?, ~기로 하다) in one paragraph.

12. Choose the correct one:

 a. 날씨가 좋은데 / 날씨가 좋구만

 b. 저는 친구를 만나기로 했어요 / 저는 친구를 만나기도 나는 것 같아요

13. Match the structure with the function:

 a. ~(으)ㄹ까요?   ( ) background or contrast

 b. ~는데   ( ) suggestion

 c. ~기로 하다   ( ) decision

14. Write a mini-dialogue using ~(으)ㄹ까요? and a polite response.

15. Fill in with ~기로 하다: 우리는 주말에 영화를 _____ 했어요.

16. Translate: Since it's raining, shall we stay home?

17. Use ~(으)ㄹ까요? in a question about eating lunch.

18. Complete the sentence: 저는 산책하기로 _____.

19. Correct the mistake: 저는 도서관에 가기로 해요.

20. Write a paragraph planning a day out with a friend using at least two of the chapter's grammar points.

Making Plans with Friends – Answer Key

1. 공원에 갈까요?

2. 저는 친구에게 전화하기로 했어요.

3. 볼까요?

4. Example: 주말에 여행을 가기로 했어요.

5. 피곤한데 산책할까요?

6. 저는 친구를 만나기로 했어요.

7. Example: 지금은 시간이 없는데 조금 이따 만날까요?

8. 할까요?

9. 날씨가 좋은데 자전거 탈까요?

10. 저녁

11. Example: 오늘은 날씨가 좋은데 밖에 나갈까요? 우리는 영화를 보기로 했어요.

12. a-날씨가 좋은데, b-만나기로 했어요

13. a- suggestion, b- background or contrast, c-decision

14. A: 오늘 영화 볼까요?

    B: 좋아요, 봐요.

15. 보기로

16. 비가 오는데 집에 있을까요?

17. 점심 먹을까요?

18. 했어요.

19. Corrected: 저는 도서관에 가기로 했어요.

20. Example: 오늘은 친구랑 함께 시간을 보내기로 했어요. "점심 먹고 공원에 갈까요?"라고 물어봤어요. 비가 오면 카페에 가기로 했어요.

Dos and Don'ts
Grammar Review

This chapter introduces essential grammar for giving instructions, prohibitions, and explaining reasons—common in polite requests and rules.

1. ~(으)면 안 된다 (must not / shouldn't)
- Used to express prohibitions.
Examples: 여기에서 담배를 피우면 안 돼요. (You must not smoke here.) / 늦으면 안 돼요. (You must not be late.)

2. ~(으)니까 (because / since)
- Used to explain reasons or provide justification.
Examples: 아프니까 쉬세요. (Since you're sick, please rest.) / 시간이 없으니까 빨리 가요. (Because there's no time, let's hurry.)

3. ~아야/어야 하다 (must / have to)
- Used to express obligation or necessity.
Examples: 약을 먹어야 해요. (You must take medicine.) / 숙제를 해야 해요. (You have to do your homework.)

These patterns are especially useful for explaining rules, giving guidance, or politely reinforcing expected behavior in everyday situations.

Exercises: Dos and Don'ts

1. Translate: You must not run here.

2. Translate: You must take your medicine.

3. Translate: Since I'm tired, I'll go home.

4. Fill in the blank with ~(으)면 안 되다: 늦_____ 안 돼요.

5. Fill in the blank with ~아야/어야 하다: 숙제를 _____ 해요.

6. Use ~(으)니까 to explain why you're eating now.

7. Use ~아야 하다 to describe what you must do today.

8. Use ~(으)면 안 되다 in a school rule sentence.

9. Translate: Because it's cold, wear a coat.

10. Translate: You must not use your phone here.

11. Rearrange: 해야 / 숙제를 / 해요 / 지금 / 저는

12. Identify the obligation: 약을 먹어야 해요.

13. Match the grammar with its function:

   a. ~(으)면 안 되다   ( ) reason

   b. ~(으)니까   ( ) prohibition

   c. ~아야 하다   ( ) obligation

14. Fill in with ~니까: 날씨가 좋_____ 산책해요.

15. Translate: You must listen to the teacher.

16. Complete: 지금 조용히 _____. (must)

17. Use all three grammar points in one paragraph.

18. Correct the mistake: 저는 학교에 가야 안 돼요.

19. Write a mini dialogue giving advice and a reason using ~아야 하다 and ~(으)니까.

20. Write a paragraph about classroom rules using at least two expressions from this chapter.

Dos and Don'ts – Answer Key

1. 여기에서 달리면 안 돼요.

2. 약을 먹어야 해요.

3. 피곤하니까 집에 갈게요.

4. 늦으면

5. 해야

6. Example: 배가 고프니까 지금 먹어요.

7. Example: 저는 오늘 은행에 가야 해요.

8. Example: 수업 시간에 떠들면 안 돼요.

9. 추우니까 코트를 입으세요.

10. 여기에서 휴대폰을 사용하면 안 돼요.

11. 저는 지금 숙제를 해야 해요.

12. Obligation: 어야 해요

13. a- prohibition, b- reason, c- obligation

14. 좋으니까

15. 선생님 말씀을 들어야 해요.

16. 해야 해요.

17. Example: 지금은 수업 시간이니까 조용히 해야 해요. 핸드폰을 보면 안 돼요.

18. Corrected: 저는 학교에 가면 안 돼요.

19. Example:

  A: 머리가 아파요.

  B: 약을 먹어야 해요. 아프니까 쉬세요.

20. Example: 교실에서는 조용히 해야 해요. 선생님 말씀을 들어야 하고, 휴대폰을 사용하면 안 돼요.

Social Etiquette
Grammar Review

This chapter introduces grammar that emphasizes respectful communication in Korean, focusing on honorifics and indirect reporting of speech.

1. ~(으)시~ (Honorific marker)
- Used to show respect when referring to someone else's actions.
- Often combined with polite endings: ~세요, ~셨습니다, etc.

Examples: 선생님께서 오셨어요. (The teacher came.) / 무엇을 드시겠어요? (What would you like to eat?)

2. ~라고 하다 (Indirect speech)
- Used to report what someone said, in either direct or paraphrased form.
- With nouns and quoted speech: [Noun] + (이)라고 하다.

Examples: 제 이름은 민수라고 해요. (My name is Minsu.) / 그는 내일 오겠다고 했어요. (He said he will come tomorrow.)

3. Rewriting for Etiquette
- Practice revising casual or neutral sentences into respectful, honorific forms.

Example: (Casual) 엄마 왔어요. → (Honorific) 어머니께서 오셨어요.

These grammar structures help learners speak more appropriately in formal situations, improve respectful tone, and report others' words clearly.

Exercises: Social Etiquette

1. Rewrite using honorifics: 선생님 왔어요.

2. Translate: What would you like to eat? (use honorifics)

3. Convert into indirect speech: 민수: "저는 학생이에요."

4. Convert into indirect speech: 엄마: "오늘 비 온대요."

5. Rewrite using ~(으)시~: 아버지가 밥을 먹어요.

6. Identify the honorific verb: 선생님께서 말씀하셨어요.

7. Use ~라고 하다 with your name introduction.

8. Rearrange into honorific form: 드세요? / 뭘 / 어머니께서

9. Fill in: 아버지께서 집에 _____. (~시다 form of 가다)

10. Match the regular verb with its honorific counterpart:

 a. 먹다   ( ) 계시다

 b. 있다   ( ) 드시다

 c. 말하다   ( ) 말씀하시다

11. Rewrite this casually spoken sentence into a respectful version: 친구 왔어요.

12. Use ~라고 하다 in a sentence where someone reports what another said.

13. Translate: He said he will come tomorrow.

14. Identify the indirect speech: 저는 민수라고 해요.

15. Correct the sentence: 아버지가 왔어요.

16. Write a short dialogue including both honorifics and indirect speech.

17. Translate: My teacher asked what I was doing.

18. Rewrite: 엄마가 잤어요. (with honorifics)

19. Fill in the indirect quote: 그는 집에 간_____ 했어요.

20. Write a paragraph introducing yourself politely and describing what someone else said about you using indirect speech.

Social Etiquette – Answer Key

1. 선생님께서 오셨어요.

2. 무엇을 드시겠어요?

3. 민수는 자신을 학생이라고 했어요.

4. 엄마가 오늘 비 온다고 했어요.

5. 아버지께서 밥을 드세요.

6. 말씀하셨어요

7. 제 이름은 [your name]라고 해요.

8. 어머니께서 뭘 드세요?

9. 가셨어요

10. a- 드시다, b- 계시다, c- 말씀하시다

11. 친구분께서 오셨어요.

12. Example: 선생님께서 내일 시험이 있다고 하셨어요.

13. 그는 내일 오겠다고 했어요.

14. 라고 해요.

15. Corrected: 아버지께서 오셨어요.

16. Example:
    A: 선생님께서는 어디 가셨어요?
    B: 집에 가신다고 하셨어요.

17. 선생님께서는 제가 뭐 하고 있는지 물으셨어요.

18. 어머님께서 주무셨어요.

19. 간다고

20. Example: 안녕하세요. 제 이름은 지수라고 해요. 선생님께서는 저를 열심히 공부하는 학생이라고 하셨어요.

School and Studies
Grammar Review

This chapter focuses on describing study habits and academic goals using patterns that express multitasking, difficulty, and purpose.

1. ~(으)면서 (while doing)

- Indicates simultaneous actions.

Examples: 저는 음악을 들으면서 공부해요. (I study while listening to music.) / 저는 친구와 이야기하면서 걷고 있어요. (I'm walking while talking with a friend.)

2. -기 쉽다 / 어렵다 (easy/difficult to do)

- Used to describe how easy or hard an action is.

Examples: 한국어 배우기 어려워요. (It's hard to learn Korean.) / 단어 외우기 쉬워요. (It's easy to memorize words.)

3. -기 위해서 (in order to)

- Used to express purpose or intent.

Examples: 저는 시험을 잘 보기 위해서 열심히 공부해요. (I study hard to do well on the test.) / 저는 한국에 가기 위해서 한국어를 배워요. (I learn Korean to go to Korea.)

These patterns are essential for talking about strategies, study goals, and everyday learning efforts in an academic context.

Exercises: School and Studies

1. Translate: I study while listening to music.

2. Translate: It's hard to concentrate.

3. Translate: I read a book while drinking coffee.

4. Use -기 위해서 to express why you study Korean.

5. Complete the sentence using ~(으)면서: 친구와 이야기_____ 걷고 있어요.

6. Use -기 쉽다 in a sentence about memorizing words.

7. Use -기 어렵다 in a sentence about grammar.

8. Translate: I practice speaking to improve my pronunciation.

9. Identify the purpose clause: 좋은 성적을 받기 위해서 공부해요.

10. Rearrange: 음악을 / 들으면서 / 공부해요 / 저는

11. Fill in: 한국어 배우_____ 어려워요.

12. Choose the correct connector (while doing): A: 운동을 <u>하면서 / 하고</u> 숙제를 했어요.

13. Match the expression with its meaning:
   a. -기 위해서   ( ) while doing
   b. ~(으)면서   ( ) to do something for a purpose
   c. -기 쉽다   ( ) easy to do

14. Translate: It is easy to use this app.

15. Use -기 위해서 in a sentence about going to the library.

16. Fill in: 시험을 잘 보_____ 열심히 공부해요.

17. Translate: Korean is difficult to speak.

18. Write a sentence using two grammar patterns from this chapter.

19. Correct the mistake: 한국어 배우는 어려워요.

20. Write a paragraph describing your study routine using at least two grammar patterns from this chapter.

School and Studies – Answer Key

1. 저는 음악을 들으면서 공부해요.

2. 집중하기 어려워요.

3. 저는 커피를 마시면서 책을 읽어요.

4. Example: 저는 한국어를 잘하기 위해서 공부해요.

5. 하면서

6. Example: 단어 외우기 쉬워요.

7. Example: 문법 이해하기 어려워요.

8. 저는 발음을 향상시키기 위해서 말하기를 연습해요.

9. 기 위해서

10. 저는 음악을 들으면서 공부해요.

11. 기

12. 하면서

13. a- to do something for a purpose, b- while doing, c- easy to do

14. 이 앱은 사용하기 쉬워요.

15. Example: 책을 빌리기 위해서 도서관에 갔어요.

16. 기 위해서

17. 한국어는 말하기 어려워요.

18. Example: 단어는 외우기 쉬워서 음악을 들으면서 공부해요.

19. Corrected: 한국어 배우기 어려워요.

20. Example: 저는 매일 아침에 음악을 들으면서 단어를 외워요. 시험을 잘 보기 위해서 열심히 공부해요. 문법은 이해하기 어려워서 복습을 많이 해요.

Health and Wellness
Grammar Review

This chapter focuses on expressing advice, sequencing, and limitations related to healthy habits and routines.

1. -(으)ㄴ 후에 (after doing)
- Used to describe what happens after an action.
Examples: 식사한 후에 운동해요. (I exercise after eating.) / 약을 먹은 후에 쉬세요. (Rest after taking medicine.)

2. -지 마세요 (please don't...)
- Used to give polite negative commands or prohibitions.
Examples: 무리하지 마세요. (Don't overdo it.) / 걱정하지 마세요. (Don't worry.)

3. -는 게 좋다 (it's good to... / you should...)
- Used to suggest or recommend actions.
Examples: 물을 많이 마시는 게 좋아요. (It's good to drink a lot of water.) / 일찍 자는 게 좋아요. (You should sleep early.)

These grammar structures help learners give and understand health-related advice, describe self-care actions, and use soft, polite directives.

Exercises: Health and Wellness

1. Translate: Rest after taking the medicine.

2. Translate: Don't worry.

3. Translate: It's good to drink warm tea.

4. Use -(으)ㄴ 후에 to describe what you do after exercise.

5. Use -지 마세요 in a polite reminder about staying up late.

6. Use -는 게 좋다 in a sentence about daily health habits.

7. Complete: 아침을 먹은 후에 _____.

8. Fill in: 너무 늦게 자_____ 마세요.

9. Choose the correct suggestion:

   a. 운동을 하는 게 좋아요 / 운동을 하지 마세요

   b. 걱정하지 마세요 / 걱정하는 게 좋아요

10. Rearrange: 쉬세요 / 후에 / 약을 / 먹은

11. Translate: After the walk, drink water.

12. Use -는 게 좋다 and -지 마세요 in one sentence.

13. Identify the sequence clause: 식사한 후에 운동해요.

14. Translate: Don't skip meals.

15. Fill in: _____는 게 좋아요. (e.g., taking vitamins)

16. Use all three grammar points in a short paragraph.

17. Correct the mistake: 밥을 먹고 후에 운동해요.

18. Translate: You should rest. Don't overdo it.

19. Write a dialogue between two friends giving each other health advice.

20. Write a paragraph about your health routine using at least two grammar points from this chapter.

Health and Wellness – Answer Key

1. 약을 먹은 후에 쉬세요.

2. 걱정하지 마세요.

3. 따뜻한 차를 마시는 게 좋아요.

4. Example: 운동한 후에 스트레칭을 해요.

5. Example: 너무 늦게 자지 마세요.

6. Example: 아침에 일찍 일어나는 게 좋아요.

7. Example: 산책해요.

8. 지

9. a-운동을 하는 게 좋아요, b-걱정하지 마세요

10. 약을 먹은 후에 쉬세요.

11. 산책한 후에 물을 마셔요.

12. Example: 무리하지 마세요. 물을 많이 마시는 게 좋아요.

13. ㄴ 후에

14. 식사를 거르지 마세요.

15. Example: 비타민을 챙겨 먹는 게 좋아요.

16. Example: 아침을 먹은 후에 운동해요. 무리하지 마세요. 물을 자주 마시는 게 좋아요.

17. Corrected: 밥을 먹은 후에 운동해요.

18. 쉬는 게 좋아요. 무리하지 마세요.

19. Example:

   A: 감기 걸렸어?

   B: 응. 약 먹은 후에 쉬려고.

   A: 그래, 무리하지 마. 물을 자주 마시는 게 좋아.

20. Example: 저는 건강을 위해 매일 아침 일찍 일어나요. 식사한 후에 산책을 하고, 무리하지 않도록 노력해요. 물을 많이 마시는 게 좋아서 자주 물을 마셔요.

Navigating Directions
Grammar Review

This chapter helps learners give and understand directions, ask questions politely, and understand spatial relationships using essential grammar.

1. ~(으)면 (if/when)

- Used for conditional statements.

Examples: 오른쪽으로 가면 은행이 있어요. (If you go right, there's a bank.) / 지하철을 타면 빨라요. (If you take the subway, it's fast.)

2. ~ㅂ/습니까? (Formal question ending)

- Polite/formal question form used in public or customer-facing speech.

Examples: 여기가 서울역입니까? (Is this Seoul Station?) / 어디에 갑니까? (Where are you going?)

3. Location Markers – ~에, ~에서, ~까지, ~으로

- Used to indicate position, origin, and destination.

Examples: 저는 학교에 갑니다. (I go to school.) / 저는 집에서 나왔어요. (I came from home.) / 저는 병원까지 걸어요. (I walk to the hospital.)

These grammar structures support confident navigation and formal interaction in unfamiliar environments or public contexts.

Exercises: Navigating Directions

1. Translate: If you go straight, you'll see a bank.

2. Translate into formal speech: Where is the station?

3. Fill in the blank with ~(으)면: 왼쪽으로 가_____ 식당이 있어요.

4. Use ~ㅂ/습니까? in a question about bus routes.

5. Identify the location marker: 집에서 학교까지 걸어요.

6. Use ~에 in a sentence about going to a location.

7. Use ~에서 in a sentence about where you started from.

8. Translate: I came from the office.

9. Rearrange: 갑니다 / 학교에 / 저는 / 아침에

10. Translate: Do you know where the pharmacy is? (formal)

11. Choose the correct conditional ending: 도서관에 가___ 책을 빌릴 수 있어요. (면/습니다)

12. Translate: If you turn right, the hospital is there.

13. Match the marker with its use:
   a. ~에   ( ) from
   b. ~에서   ( ) to
   c. ~까지   ( ) at/in/to

14. Write a sentence combining ~(으)면 and ~에.

15. Fill in the blank using formal speech: 이 버스는 학교까지 _____? (to go)

16. Use all three location markers in one sentence.

17. Translate: I'm going to the bank from the park.

18. Correct the mistake: 병원에서 갑니다 집에.

19. Write a short dialogue asking and giving directions using formal speech.

20. Write a paragraph describing how to get to your favorite restaurant using direction grammar from this chapter.

Navigating Directions – Answer Key

1. 똑바로 (or 쭉) 가면 은행이 보여요.

2. 역이 어디에 있습니까?

3. 면

4. 이 버스는 어디로 갑니까?

5. ~에서, ~까지

6. Example: 도서관에 갑니다.

7. Example: 집에서 출발했어요.

8. 저는 회사에서 왔어요.

9. 저는 아침에 학교에 갑니다.

10. 약국이 어디에 있는지 아십니까?

11. 면

12. 오른쪽으로 돌면 병원이 있어요.

13. a- at/in/to, b- from, c- to

14. Example: 학교에 가면 도서관도 있어요.

15. 갑니까

16. Example: 저는 집에서 출발해서 은행에 갔다가 시장까지 걸었어요.

17. 저는 공원에서 은행으로 가요.

18. Corrected: 병원에서 집으로 갑니다.

19. A: 은행이 어디에 있습니까?

　 B: 똑바로 (or 쭉) 가면 오른쪽에 있습니다.

20. Example: 집에서 나와서 왼쪽으로 도세요. 큰 길까지 걸으면 식당이 있어요. 식당에 도착하면 바로 보입니다.

Banking and Finance
Grammar Review

This chapter introduces grammar patterns that are especially useful for handling financial transactions, asking for services, and clarifying procedures.

1. ~(으)려고 (in order to / intend to)
- Used to express the purpose of an action.
Examples: 저는 돈을 찾으려고 은행에 갔어요. (I went to the bank to withdraw money.) / 저는 계좌를 만들려고 합니다. (I intend to open an account.)

2. -면 되다 (it's enough to... / you just need to...)
- Used to indicate sufficient action or conditions.
Examples: 여권을 보여주면 돼요. (You just need to show your passport.) / 이 서류에 서명하면 됩니다. (It's enough to sign this document.)

These patterns help navigate common banking tasks politely and efficiently by clearly stating intentions and understanding instructions.

Exercises: Banking and Finance

1. Translate: I went to the bank to exchange money.

2. Translate: You just need to bring your ID.

3. Use ~(으)려고 in a sentence about opening an account.

4. Fill in the blank with -면 되다: 서명하_____ 됩니다.

5. Use -면 되다 in a sentence about applying for a card.

6. Rearrange into a correct sentence: 가요 / 은행에 / 저는 / 돈을 / 보내려고

7. Use ~(으)려고 with the verb '찾다' (to withdraw).

8. Translate: I came to the bank to pay the bill.

9. Choose the correct form:

  a. 신청하려고 해요 / 신청면 돼요

  b. 확인하려고 합니다 / 확인면 됩니다

10. Identify the expression of intent: 계좌를 만들려고 해요.

11. Fill in: 여권을 보여주_____ 돼요.

12. Translate: I just need to write my name here.

---

13. Use both ~(으)려고 and -면 되다 in one sentence.

14. Match the expression to its meaning:

  a. ~(으)려고   ( ) You just need to...

  b. -면 되다   ( ) In order to...

15. Translate: You just need to press this button.

16. Write a question using -면 됩니까? in a banking setting.

17. Correct the mistake: 이 서류를 제출하려고 되다.

18. Use ~(으)려고 in a formal sentence about making a deposit.

19. Fill in: 통장을 _____ 은행에 왔어요. (to update the bankbook)

20. Write a paragraph describing a visit to the bank using both grammar patterns from this chapter.

Banking and Finance – Answer Key

1. 저는 돈을 바꾸려고 은행에 갔어요.

2. 신분증만 가져오면 돼요.

3. 저는 계좌를 만들려고 합니다.

4. 면

5. 카드 신청서만 작성하면 돼요.

6. 저는 돈을 보내려고 은행에 가요.

7. Example: 돈을 찾으려고 은행에 갔어요.

8. 저는 요금을 내려고 은행에 왔어요.

9. a-신청하려고 해요, b-확인하려고 합니다

10. 려고 해요

11. 면

12. 여기에 이름만 쓰면 돼요.

13. Example: 계좌를 만들려고 은행에 간다면, 신분증만 있으면 돼요.

14. a- In order to..., b- You just need to...

15. 이 버튼만 누르면 돼요.

16. Example: 여권만 있으면 됩니까?

17. Corrected: 이 서류를 제출하려고 합니다.

18. 입금하려고 합니다.

19. 정리하려고

20. Example: 오늘 은행에 갔어요. 돈을 찾으려고 갔고, 계좌를 열기 위해 상담을 받았어요. 서류를 제출하면 된다고 했어요.

Mail and Delivery
Grammar Review

This chapter focuses on language used in mailing, delivery, and customer transactions, emphasizing formal requests and methods of service.

1. ~(으)로 (by/with/toward)

- Used to indicate method, direction, or means of sending.

Examples: 우편으로 보내세요. (Send it by mail.) / 택배로 받았어요. (I received it by delivery.)

2. -(으)십시오 (formal polite command/request)

- High-level politeness, used in public service and official instructions.

Examples: 여기에 주소를 적으십시오. (Please write your address here.) / 기다리십시오. (Please wait.)

3. Transaction Expressions (using formal language in service settings)

Examples: 무엇을 보내시겠습니까? (What would you like to send?) / 영수증을 받으시겠습니까? (Would you like a receipt?) / 이 양식을 작성하십시오. (Please fill out this form.)

These patterns are essential for handling postal tasks, filling out forms, and interacting in formal delivery or mailing environments.

Exercises: Mail and Delivery

1. Translate: Please write your name here. (formal)

2. Translate: I received the package by delivery.

3. Use ~(으)로 in a sentence about sending mail.

4. Fill in the blank with -(으)십시오: 문을 _____. (to open)

5. Translate: Would you like a receipt? (formal)

6. Use -(으)십시오 in a sentence giving instructions.

7. Rearrange into a correct sentence: 보내십시오 / 우편으로 / 이것을

8. Use ~(으)로 with a vehicle or delivery method.

9. Identify the polite command: 주소를 적으십시오.

10. Translate: Send it by registered mail.

11. Fill in: 영수증을 _____습니까? (to receive, formal)

12. Choose the correct polite form:

  a. 여기에 이름을 적으세요 / 적으십시오

  b. 이것을 주세요 / 주십시오

13. Use both ~(으)로 and -(으)십시오 in one sentence.

14. Translate: Please wait in line.

15. Match the form to its use:

  a. ~(으)로 _____ ( ) polite request

  b. -(으)십시오 _____ ( ) direction or means

16. Use a transaction expression in a complete sentence.

17. Translate: I sent the letter by air mail.

18. Correct the mistake: 이것을 보내요 우편으로.

19. Write a short dialogue at the post office using polite forms.

20. Write a paragraph about sending a package using grammar from this chapter.

Mail and Delivery – Answer Key

1. 여기에 이름을 적으십시오.

2. 택배로 받았어요.

3. Example: 편지를 우편으로 보냈어요.

4. 여십시오.

5. 영수증을 받으시겠습니까?

6. Example: 이 양식을 작성하십시오.

7. 이것을 우편으로 보내십시오.

8. Example: 소포를 택배로 보냈어요.

9. 으십시오.

10. 등기로 보내십시오.

11. 받으시겠

12. a-적으십시오, b-주십시오

13. Example: 이 양식을 우편으로 보내십시오.

14. 줄을 서서 기다리십시오.

15. a- direction or means, b- polite request

16. Example: 무엇을 보내시겠습니까?

17. 편지를 항공우편으로 보냈어요.

18. Corrected: 이것을 우편으로 보내요.

19. A: 무엇을 보내시겠습니까?

　B: 이 서류를 등기로 보내고 싶습니다.

　A: 이 양식을 작성하십시오.

20. Example: 저는 지난주에 친구에게 선물을 보냈어요. 우편으로 보내고 싶어서 우체국에 갔어요. 직원이 이 양식을 작성하라고 하셨어요. 줄을 서서 기다린 후, 등기로 보냈어요.

Talking About the Weather
Grammar Review

This chapter reviews grammar for describing weather, giving contrast, and expressing potential or conditional actions.

1. ~(으)ㄹ 수 있다/없다 (can/cannot)
- Used to express ability or possibility.
Examples: 저는 밖에 나갈 수 있어요. (I can go outside.) / 눈이 많이 와서 저는 운전할 수 없어요. (It's snowing a lot, so I can't drive.)

2. ~(으)려면 (if you intend to / in order to)
- Expresses conditional intent; what must be done to accomplish something.
Examples: 여행을 가려면 미리 예약해야 해요. (If you want to travel, you have to book in advance.) / 등산하려면 날씨가 좋아야 해요. (To go hiking, the weather must be good.)

3. ~지만 (but / although)
- Used to contrast two clauses.
Examples: 춥지만 저는 밖에 나가요. (It's cold, but I'm going outside.) / 비가 오지만 우리는 축구를 했어요. (It was raining, but we played soccer.)

These patterns allow learners to describe the weather clearly, explain conditional plans, and contrast weather-related expectations with actual events.

Exercises: Talking About the Weather

1. Translate: I can go outside.

2. Translate: I can't go hiking because it's raining.

3. Use ~(으)려면 in a sentence about going to the beach.

4. Fill in the blank with 나가다 and ~(으)ㄹ 수 없다: 비가 와서 밖에 _____ .

5. Use ~지만 to contrast cold weather and playing soccer.

6. Use ~(으)ㄹ 수 있다 in a sentence about driving in snow.

7. Translate: If you want to go hiking, the weather must be good.

8. Rearrange into a correct sentence: 춥지만 / 나가요 / 밖에/ 저는

9. Fill in: 눈이 많이 오면 운전할 수 _____.

10. Use all three grammar points in one paragraph.

11. Identify the conditional clause: 비가 오면 못 가요.

12. Translate: It's sunny but cold.

13. Write a conditional sentence: To go to the park, the weather must be nice.

14. Correct the mistake: 날씨가 좋아면 산책할 수 있어요.

15. Match the expression to its function:

   a. ~(으)ㄹ 수 있다   ( ) contrast

   b. ~(으)려면   ( ) ability/possibility

   c. ~지만   ( ) conditional intent

16. Translate: We wanted to go out, but it rained.

17. Use ~(으)ㄹ 수 없다 in a formal sentence.

18. Fill in: 해가 나지만 날씨가 _____. (cold)

19. Write a dialogue about planning a picnic, using weather-related contrast and conditions.

20. Write a paragraph describing a change of plans due to weather using at least two grammar points from this chapter.

Talking About the Weather – Answer Key

1. 저는 밖에 나갈 수 있어요.

2. 비가 와서 저는 등산할 수 없어요.

3. Example: 해변에 가려면 수영복을 가져와야 해요.

4. 나갈 수 없어요.

5. Example: 날씨가 춥지만 축구를 해요.

6. 눈이 와도 운전할 수 있어요.

7. 등산하려면 날씨가 좋아야 해요.

8. 집에 있지만 나가요.

9. 없어요

10. Example: 날씨가 춥지만 밖에 나갈 수 있어요. 바다로 여행을 가려면 미리 예약해야 해요.

11. 비가 오면

12. 맑지만 추워요.

13. 공원에 가려면 날씨가 좋아야 해요.

14. Corrected: 날씨가 좋으면 산책할 수 있어요.

15. a- ability/possibility, b- conditional intent, c- contrast

16. 우리는 나가고 싶었지만 비가 왔어요.

17. 눈이 많이 와서 운전할 수 없습니다.

18. 춥습니다. (or 추워요.)

19. A: 내일 소풍 갈까요?
    B: 좋아요. 하지만 비가 오면 못 가요.
    A: 맞아요. 비가 오지 않으면 갈 수 있어요.

20. Example: 우리는 공원에 가려고 했어요. 하지만 비가 와서 갈 수 없었어요. 다음 주에 가려면 그 날에 날씨가 좋아야 해요.

Thank You!

Thank you again for choosing my book!

You are now well on your way to mastering the Korean language. By completing these exersizes you now know where you need to study more to reinforce where you need to focus. After studying, go through the questions again and see how you improce.

If you enjoyed studying Korean with us, we would very much like to hear about your progress in a review where you purchased this book.

We are always eager to learn if there is anything we can do to make our books better for future students. We are committed to making the best language learning content available! Please do get in touch with us via email if you had a problem withany of the content in this book:

hello@polyscholar.com

Visit www.polyscholar.com to pick up my first book <u>Learn Korean for Beginners</u> and our other language books.

Thank You

Thank You